Thirty Years in Forced Labor Camps:

Memoir of a Survivor

Wang Pizhong

Translated by Emma Tao White
and Steven C. White

Remembering Publishing, LLC

Copyright © 2022 by Remembering Publishing, LLC. USA

Thirty Years in Forced Labor Camp:

Memoir of a Survivor

Wang Pizhong

Translated by Emma Tao White and Steven C. White

Executive Editor: Fu Qiang
Illustrator: Hu Jie

ISBN: 978-1-68560-040-2 (Print)
978-1-68560-041-9 (eBook)

LCCN: 2022 905474

2022.4, First Edition; First Printing

Remembering Publishing, LLC
RememPub@gmail.com

All rights reserved.
No part of this book may be reproduced in any form or by any electronic or mechanical means including information storage and retrieval systems, without permission in writing from the publisher. The only exception is by a reviewer, who may quote short excerpts in review.

Wang Pizhong, Beijing Xiangshan Botanical Garden, 2007

PREFACE

I spent thirty years in captivity. The first sentence I served was twelve years of *laogai,* "reform through labor".[1] The next eighteen years, referred to as the "second reform through labor", were a "voluntary" continuation of the same work.

In 1949, at the time of the Communist takeover, I was working at the Shanghai Bureau of Direct Taxation, under the Ministry of Finance.[2] Afterward, I stayed on. At the end of January 1951, I was arrested for being a spy.[3] Thereafter, I endured numerous ordeals. After a few months, I was moved to a detention center on Station Street, then to Tilanchiao Prison Compound, the largest prison in Shanghai. In the name of reeducation and reform, I was coerced to accuse others of wrongdoing that never happened and to disclose confidential information about people I knew. A year later, I was sentenced by the Shanghai Municipal Military Control Committee to twelve years in a labor prison camp.

In 1963, when my sentence was up, my release turned into another round of hard labor. Everyone due for discharge was coerced into signing

---

1 Laogai (simplified Chinese:劳改; traditional Chinese:勞改; pinyin: Láogǎi) is the abbreviation for Láodòng Gǎizào (simplified Chinese:劳动改造; traditional Chinese: 勞動改造), which means reform through labor. Laogai is a criminal justice system involving the use of penal labor and prison farms in communist states including People's Republic of China (PRC) and North Korea (DPRK).

2 The military force of the Communist Party of China (CPC) defeated the army of the Nationalist Party of China (NPC) and took over Shanghai on May 27th, 1949. The author was initially employed by the Shanghai Bureau of Direct Taxation when NPC ruled Shanghai.

3 CPC built its party-state after the defeat of NPC in China's Civil War during 1945-1949. On October 1st, 1949, CPC held a ceremony in Beijing to officially announce the establishment of the People's Republic of China. However, the newly established republic was challenged by rebels, revolts and war threats both inside and outside China. Ensuing political campaigns initiated by CPC aimed to smash confrontational forces and to hunt enemies. The author was mis-recognized and unfairly sentenced as a spy in one of the earliest political campaigns, the Suppressing Counter-revolutionary Campaign.

the "Voluntary Request to Remain." From the Reform through Labor Camp we were sent to a nearby Workers Camp to continue our farm work. Those who refused to sign were considered insufficiently rehabilitated and their sentences were expediently extended.

There were some differences between the prison laborers and the "discharged" workers: 1) The prisoners were confined within a walled compound surrounded by armed guards, while the workers lived in unguarded dorms outside the walled compound. 2) Prisoners received no stipend while "discharged" workers received a small stipend. 3) While workers still ate at a communal facility, they were required to manage their own food and clothing. 4) Prisoners were not allowed any leaves, while workers could apply for home visits, even though the chance of receiving one was practically nil.

Prisoners and "discharged" workers had more similarities than differences. Both groups had been deprived of their civil rights. Prison laborers were considered criminals, while workers were classified as one of the Four Undesirables – the landlords, the rich, the counterrevolutionaries, and the wicked. Both were required to toil endlessly. Both were subjected to harsh discipline. There were rules for the daily routine, rules for study sessions, etc. Violators were subjected to various punishments. Those who were found or suspected of escaping, listening to unfriendly broadcasts, plotting a rebellion, disputing socialism, or making disrespectful remarks about revolutionary leaders were severely punished. Medical care was woefully inadequate. In most cases, sick leave was rarely granted. In short, we worked under unbearable conditions.

During my second reform through labor sentence I witnessed many tragic events, especially during the Cultural Revolution.4 After the death of Mao Zedong and the downfall of the Gang of Four, workers were no longer labeled as one of the undesirables, and were able to regain some civil rights.5 In 1979 I was released from captivity after thirty years, and

---

4 The Cultural Revolution, formally known as the Great Proletarian Cultural Revolution, was a Maoist sociopolitical campaign in China. Mao embarked on his last revolutionary endeavor, the Cultural Revolution, in 1966, and his death in 1976 marked the closure of this campaign.

5 The Gang of Four (simplified Chinese: 四人帮; traditional Chinese: 四人幫; pinyin: Sì rén bāng) was a Maoist political faction composed of four CPC officials. They came to prominence during the Cultural Revolution and under CPC's post-Mao rule, they were charged with a series of treasonous crimes.

went to work as an English teacher in a high school set up by the Reform through Labor Bureau. Most of the students were children of the Bureau's cadres and staff. I returned to society after a 30-year hiatus.

At the time of my arrest, I had an elder brother and a sister-in-law. Counting my parents, it was a family of five. A niece was born during my imprisonment. War and other factors hindered my getting married. By the time I visited my hometown after my discharge, my family had passed away except for my niece who had married. I felt like a solitary and pitiful soul.

After the Cultural Revolution, the government went to great lengths to exonerate the many unjust and false prosecutions. Many of my friends were exonerated through appeals. To me, it made more sense not to acquiesce to a totalitarian government. I was prepared to be labeled a counterrevolutionary for the rest of my life regardless of how it would affect my welfare.

As the political climate in the country gradually changed, more and more people were exonerated. Even though I had regained my civil rights, I was still labeled a counterrevolutionary. I could bear the stigma, but it cast a shadow on those around me. The school that hired me, my friends, and even my acquaintances faced gloomy prospects and potential political disadvantages. Therefore, I changed my mind and sent in my appeal. Because it was a simple case with no accomplices, the process was relatively short. A little over a year after I filed the petition, the court declared me exonerated; I was no longer labeled a counterrevolutionary. The office I had worked in prior to my arrest granted me a small pension, just enough for me to get by on.

Even though vindication came in 1979, my writing of this account did not start until 1989. I hesitated because I did not have confidence in my writing ability and I thought that another victim of unjust imprisonment and forced labor must surely have already written such an account. Many victims of the Communist takeover and the Cultural Revolution urged me to chronicle my thirty years. But I was undecided.

At a party in 1988, many of the guests had passed through the afflictions of the Cultural Revolution. Some were implicated and others were entrapped. Still others had miserable experiences in prison. All of them vented grievances and talked about how they were labeled rightists and counterrevolutionaries. I became indignant. In this setting, I also related my horrific experiences in the labor camps. Much of it they had never heard of. Many found it unbelievable. They persuaded me to write it down. But I was still undecided.

Later, I read two novels about labor camps. These romanticized descriptions of camp life bore little resemblance to what I experienced. The only narrative on prison life that I came across was a translation of *I Was a Prisoner of Mao Zedong*, by a French missionary who was charged with espionage.[6] But his treatment as a foreigner was vastly different from mine. A story similar to mine had not yet been written; I, therefore, decided to document the inhumane and unjust treatment I endured. No matter how modest my account, it would be a persuasive argument for the struggle for human rights and a just government, showing that a government ruled by one person could only lead to corruption and terror.

Nevertheless, I was already at an advanced age and in frail health. During my years of servitude, I had withstood many adversities. If I did not create any trouble now, I could subsist for the rest of my life in peace. But if I disclosed my 30-year ordeal, would I face another round of torture and abuse? Recalling the decades of political persecution in China, I was fearful of chronicling those years. Although this fear was a formidable deterrent, I decided that I must record what happened to me.

The years of forced labor, the death of family members, and my now gloomy solitary existence had consolidated into bitterness. Writing about my thirty years in captivity would allow me to let go of this bitterness and have some inner peace. It would provide a historical record for future generations. Whatever misfortune I might face because of these disclosures became less of a concern.

When I began to write, I found it painful to resurrect the past. This process took over all aspects of my life—while eating, strolling, and in bed. What was blurred from the distant past became clearer, what was forgotten reappeared vividly. These memories accentuated my sorrow and anger to an almost unbearable degree, but the process of writing finally brought me some measure of peace.

Because of my experiences, I've come to understand that there is nothing as treacherous and cruel as political persecution. It affects the greatest number of people. When I was accused of being a spy, I could not

---

6 Chelminski, Rudolph (Bao, Ruo-Wang). *Prisoners of Mao*. New York Coward, McCann & Geoghegan, 1973. Chelminski's memoir was translated and published by a Chinese publishing house (Tianjin Qiushi Publishing House, 天津求实出版社) in 1989.

adequately defend myself since others did not know for sure whether I was guilty or not. No one dared to suggest a thorough investigation or give me a hand in the name of justice. No one dared to sympathize with me, let alone defend me. Anyone attempting to come to my aid would have been deemed guilty by association. After thirty years of forced labor, I was old and weak with failing health, a life destroyed by political oppression. Even if I wanted to be vengeful, there was no clear adversary I could target.

CONTENTS

PREFACE	I
CHAPTER 1 THE BEGINNING	1
Liuyong	2
Activists	3
Preparing to Leave for Hong Kong	6
The Arrest	9
CHAPTER 2 IMPRISONMENT AND PRELIMINARY TRIALS	12
Beginning of the Arrest	13
Life in Jail	15
Charged with a Crime	18
Station Road Detention House	22
The Verdict	26
The Red Police Truck	29
CHAPTER 3 TILANQIAO PRISON	31
Gunshots Outside the Window	32
Prison Uproar	34
The Sentence	35
Re-sentencing	38
CHAPTER 4 FIXING THE HUAI RIVER IN NORTHERN ANHUI	40
Thrown into Reform through Labor	41
Excavation Work at the Huai River	45
The Move to Northern Jiangsu Province	49
CHAPTER 5 FARM WORK IN NORTHERN JIANGSU	51
From Wasteland to Cotton Fields	52
Words that Led to Disaster	56
Escape Plans	59

Injury	61
Expose the Rebels	63

CHAPTER 6 RAILROAD WORK IN THE WEST — 71

Bawang River Bridge	72
Food Rationing	75
55 Kilometers	79
Group Evaluation	82
39 Kilometers	85
Hangman's Pass	87

CHAPTER 7 FARMING IN BAOANZHAO, INNER MONGOLIA — 90

Repair Dry Dam	91
Big New Farm	96
Flood Season	98
Harsh Winter	101
The Great Leap Forward	102
"Appeal" and Re-sentence	104
"Voluntary Request to Remain"	108

CHAPTER 8 FARM WORKER PERIOD — 113

Work Points	114
Four Clarification Campaign	116
The Three Allegiances	118
Denunciation Campaign	120
Commissar Wang	124
Cultural Revolution's Aftermath	125

CHAPTER 9 APPEAL AND EXONERATION — 127

End of the Cultural Revolution	128
Appeal	129
Exoneration	131

AFTERWORD — 133

CHAPTER 1

THE BEGINNING

LIUYONG

Liuyong, "retained on the job", was a term coined by the Communists, specifically referring to those who had been employed by the Nationalist government but kept on the job after the takeover. Most were in the middle or lower echelon, unimportant militarily or politically.

In the fall of 1948, the Communist Liberation Army had successive victories in northeastern China. The Nationalist Army retreated in a disorderly manner to the south of Shanhai Pass. In the spring of 1949, the Liberation Army stormed into the Xuzhou area. Thus began the famous Huaihai Battle, a decisive victory for the Liberation Army.1 Because of the strategic importance of that theater, the Nationalists lost their will to fight and dispersed. The Communists would soon come to power.

At the time, I was a staff member of the Shanghai Bureau of Direct Taxation, an office directly under the Ministry of Finance. I joined the office not through personal contacts but by passing a qualifying examination for financial and administrative personnel. Those of us titled "Trained Qualified Personnel" formed the core of the Ministry's staff. We were not affected by supervisory changes or reorganization.

At a critical moment a friendly colleague, with contacts in the inner circle, confided to me that danger was imminent. The government was planning to move to Taiwan. If I wanted to go, he could arrange it. He advised me to prepare early. I asked whether families could go along. He said, "No, because there would not be enough transportation for that many people." One had to go first and move the family over later.

I worried that if I left my current job, I might not get another one. If I went to Taiwan, I would not be able to support my parents on the Mainland. Moreover, the Nationalists had proven to be corrupt and

---

1 During the Chinese Civil War, CPC reorganized its army and renamed this the new million-strong force the "People's Liberation Army" (PLA). CPC retained this name of its army after its all-encompassing victory over the Nationalist Party in 1949 and the establishment of a new republic in the same year.

incompetent. Despite having millions of soldiers, they had lost ground to the Communists. After fleeing to a tiny island with a small population, the defeated troops could face an even more difficult task of defending themselves. If I followed them and the Communists captured Taiwan, I would have nowhere to retreat. So I concluded that fleeing to Taiwan was worse than staying where I was. Since I had done nothing against the Communists, I had nothing to fear under its regime. I decided to stay.

In the summer of 1949, Shanghai was liberated by the Communists. I was hopeful that political unrest, job insecurity, price instability, and ideological contention would become a thing of the past, and that we would have the opportunity to build a new and better China. The Nationalists were defeated; Mao and the Communist Party would now run the country. Since I had not contributed to this historic event, I felt dwarfed and ashamed in front of the newcomers.

Life in the workplace quickly changed. Retained personnel had to attend reeducation sessions. Before being deployed to a new post, everyone was required to demonstrate his political leanings and be thoroughly investigated, as well as learn revolutionary theory, Party policy, and new office procedures. My original office was restructured under a new name. I was transferred to another office. Although I was not pleased with this development, all I could do was to make a fresh start, to work cheerfully and diligently for a brighter future.

I did not approve of the Kuomintang government, and instead cherished the same dream as the Communists. I thought that Communism must be superior, that it would be instrumental in getting rid of the many shortcomings inherent in capitalism, thereby promoting social progress and bringing good fortune to all the people. But my dream of this glorious future under Communism was soon destroyed by their bizarre policies and perverse political campaigns.

ACTIVISTS

I began my new position in the fall of 1949. At first, the office was made up mostly of retained staff. Working relationships were amicable. Shortly thereafter, many new younger cadres were sent in. We were to look upon them as the backbone of the office. They were described as "activists," signifying that they were hard-working and ideologically sound. We were told to follow their example.

My immediate supervisor, Mr. Xieh, was one of these "activists." Prejudiced, arbitrary, and despotic, he treated the retained employees like captives. He often met with the activists and excluded the retained workers. We were not to express our opinions but were expected to blindly obey. Under these circumstances, the retained staff would occasionally vent our resentment among each other but took great care not to divulge our feelings to the others. When speaking, we carefully weighed our words and tone of voice to avoid offending anyone. Meanwhile, they scrutinized our every word and gesture. Sometimes they even feigned sympathy in order to solicit reactionary remarks, then report us so as to gain favor with the supervisor. It was in that type of trap when I was caught off-guard and said, "It looks like instead of being liberated, we were captured."

After the words came out, there was an ominous moment of silence. I immediately sensed that I had made a disastrous slip of the tongue. I was upset because I knew I could be in peril, and worried about it for many days. After a few quiet days, I felt a little easier. But the question remained as to whether my remark had been overlooked.

There is an old Chinese saying, "Do not frighten the snakes away while beating the grass to capture a small creature." First, they covertly collect all the material against you, and attack when you are least prepared to defend yourself. They could care less about the authenticity of the material. Since verification takes time and effort, it was seldom done. Sometimes, the person charged with the investigation resorts to forgery or fabrication. Whenever I thought about this, I was gripped with fear. At first, I did not know whether I had been secretly reported for my imprudent utterance. Then judging from the increasing discrimination and oppression, I undoubtedly was.

A retained worker, who has been put under surveillance and characterized as a counterrevolutionary, would rarely be viewed differently again. The judicial offices bragged that their targets would not be able to escape from its powerful security network. I was working and living in an unbearable environment of terror and distrust. But there was nothing I could do.

One day a meeting was held to arrange work assignments. During the meeting, the activists made a lot of suggestions. Since none of them thought about applying rules, I made a proposal. As my words were being uttered, I was loudly attacked. I was reproached for lacking the correct viewpoint. Mr. Xieh, who was presiding over the meeting and always sided with the activists, kept silent. The young activists, most of whom had no education beyond high school, were more interested in attacking me than in judging the merits of my proposal. They dispensed with a rational analysis of my proposal by shouting, "Long Live Chairman Mao." This was only the beginning of how I was to be treated.

After this incident, a fellow retained worker and friend advised me to be more discreet. At that moment, I did not fully appreciate his well-intentioned advice. I felt that I had the right to express what I thought and that I had been correct. As long as I knew that I was not a conspirator or agent, I had no reason to hide my opinions. I did not recognize the precarious situation I was in and adhere to the adage, "Be careful in speech and judicious in action." I was foolish for not giving self-preservation top priority.

During the winter of 1949, staff members were called upon to make pledges on a government bond. More than half of those at the meeting were activists. Supervisor Xieh announced that everyone was to make a pledge. The amount would then be approved by the group and recorded. I had no idea how much I should pledge. With a small income, I could not afford to make a generous pledge. I planned to follow the crowd.

When Mr. Xieh asked, "Who will make the first pledge?" Immediately, someone proposed that I be the first. The whole crowd shouted in agreement. So much for my plan to follow the crowd.

Feeling trapped, I said "I don't know how much to pledge. Too little is not good. Too much is beyond my means. Could someone else go first?"

One of the activists responded, "If everyone made the same excuse, who would go first? As to how much you should pledge, the more, the better. Why don't you rise to the occasion?"

Xieh interjected with a cold and harsh tone, "You are one of the more senior members. How could you not set an example for the younger ones?"

Xieh was an opportunist who had previously deserted the Party, only to rejoin after the Party came to power. I had been advised to be on guard against his treachery. Rather than refute him, I immediately pledged an amount, hoping that I had met my obligation. At the time, the amount was a burden for me.

As soon as I pledged, someone retorted, "Only that much? We know you have money. You should pledge at least XX Composite Units." The currency situation was in a state of transition. One "Composite Unit" was equivalent to 6,000 of the inflated, then defunct, Nationalist currency.

"I am in a very difficult position. I do not have much money," I replied.

"Who's going to believe you? You are stained with the vices of the bourgeoisie—selfishness and miserliness." Following this remark, all the other activists joined in. I was furious but managed to control my temper and said, "Is the pledge voluntary or mandatory?" I turned around and asked Xieh. He gave no answer, did not look at me, and turned away with a sardonic grin. He stated ominously, "Let him be. The Communist Party and the People's Government will not crumble because of his miserly pledge."

He implied that I cared more about my money than the government. I was so furious that I wanted to walk away. But I saw that if I were labeled as a saboteur, the consequences would be dire. Then the others pledged. Mostly of the same amount, probably agreed upon earlier. After each pledge, the group shouted, "Approved." In the end, the registrar asked, "Does anyone else want to pledge?" I said, "I have not pledged yet. I want to pledge X Units." The registrar hesitated. He looked at Xieh, who said nothing. I urged the registrar to take down my amount and he finally did. The meeting adjourned after some brief instructions.

I left the meeting feeling angry, fearful, and confused, wondering how I could stand up to such ordeals. Little did I know of the decades of devastation to come.

PREPARING TO LEAVE FOR HONG KONG

From that point on, my situation became even more unbearable. My work was frequently scrutinized and criticized, usually without any basis. Another devious move was to assign me to inspect various industries. As I later discovered, they secretly followed me. I was angry but not afraid;

since I was not a spy, I had nothing to hide.

One day, I realized someone was following me. I turned around and tried to chase him but he fled. One summer night, while taking a walk in Chungsan Park, I heard someone in the bushes. When I peeked in, two people immediately hid. Another time, while mailing a letter at the post office, I noticed someone was watching me closely. I left and returned quickly. The same person was now in the work area, asking the clerk to open the mailbox to see to whom I had sent my letter.

Added to these conditions were my financial woes. Everyone in the office except me was reclassified and received salary increases. My salary of 120 Composite Units was not nearly enough for me and my parents to live on. I had to borrow money to subsist. But that year, nearly all my relatives and friends were stressed financially and could not lend me anything.

At that time, a hard, painful lump appeared in my left breast. After a few visits to the hospital and several ineffective injections, I turned to traditional Chinese medicine. I was told that the lump was the result of mental distress and stagnation of blood and energy. Fortunately, after being treated with herbal broth and plasters, the lump went away in a couple of weeks.

Although my body was healed, I was tormented by my situation. A friendly colleague—a party member who had access to the inner circle—told me that a proposal had been made to openly criticize me at a meeting. The proposal failed only because Bureau Chief Wang did not like that form of reeducation.

One day in the winter of 1950 I ran into a college friend, Mr. Chang, at a tram stop. He had just returned from Beijing. He had left his job because he could no longer bear the subversion and discrimination of his new colleagues. When I told him of my troubles, we found that we were going through the same torment and empathized with each other. During our next visits, we discussed our future. We felt that there was no chance for us to live in peace under this new regime. It was impossible for people who cherished democracy and human rights to adapt to a totalitarian government. He told me that an American professor from the Department of Economics of our college, Yenching University, was now in charge of the Asia and Pacific office of the UNRRA. His office moved to Okinawa after the overthrow but had a branch in Hong Kong. Many classmates had joined him. My friend planned to go, and asked if I would go with him. With my situation at the office and my dire financial straits,

I saw this as the only way out and said yes.

During the early stage of Communist rule, people looked abroad for relief. Hong Kong was the closest and most convenient destination. Not only was the fare low, but no traveling papers or visa was required. One of my relatives operated a successful poultry farm in Yuanlong, a suburb of Hong Kong. Before the Liberation they had invited my mother and me to visit. If I went now, I could stay with them while I looked for a job. Of course, my hope was to have the American professor find me a job at the UNRRA.

After deciding to go to Hong Kong, I visited my parents and explained everything to them. Except for what I needed for the trip, I gave my parents what little savings I had. The responsibility for taking care of my parents fell upon my elder brother. The hope was that my exit will enable me to help the whole family later.

When I returned to Shanghai the next morning, I found that all my belongings had been ransacked. I asked the attendant who had done it. At first, he did not want to say. After I pressed him repeatedly, he revealed who the two men might have been. Since the Communist takeover, there were frequent reports of "exposing" counterrevolutionary "hideouts." Executions were common events, but nobody knew that at the time.

I was suspected of being an agent of the rebels because of my rather obstinate and forthright nature. My "crime" was not being submissive enough during the last year and a half. I did not pretend to support the Party. Sometimes, I even made statements contrary to their official position. I behaved that way, not because I was unable to "toe the line," but because I did not want to. Under the circumstances, even if I were not classified as an agent, they would at least consider me a class dissident. In the eyes of the power elite, the presence of such elements could obstruct their power or spark their disintegration. The ensuing campaigns—"Suppress the Opposition," "Campaign against the Three Evils," "Campaign against the Five Evils," "Anti-Rightist Campaign," "Purge the Counterrevolutionaries," and the Cultural Revolution—were all for the purpose of repression.

Chapter 1 *The Beginning*

THE ARREST

In early 1951, I sold my radio, my watch, and some of my clothes, and borrowed some money to pay for my fare. I knew I would not become a vagabond on the streets of Hong Kong since I had a relative there. At that time, to go to Hong Kong, all one had to do was to state a reason and apply for a pass. Since I had a cousin in Hong Kong, I used her address and applied for a visiting permit. But the college friend who was supposed to go with me had an unexpected problem. One day in mid-December, he told me that his wife was at her home in Beijing and that he must get her consent and procure more money for the trip. Even though I was anxious to leave, I had to wait for him to return.

In late December, I went to the Personnel Office and told them that I could no longer work in that office and asked them to let me resign. I said I would find another job after my health recovered. Their answer was, "The Bureau has no rules for resigning. If you have a health problem, you may go to a government hospital for an examination. The office will grant you a sick leave upon a doctor's certification." Rebuffed, I sadly returned to my room, calculating the risk of leaving without formal severance. Since I was already under surveillance and left without going through the proper channels, they might think I was fleeing and arrest me. So I decided to be patient.

Toward the end of January 1951, I received a notice to report to the Personnel Office. As a reactionary under surveillance, I knew I was likely to be punished. The Personnel Office was at another location. I arrived there at noon.

"Why did you call me in?" I asked.

"Did you want to resign?" he asked me.

"Yes," I said, "for health reasons. I'm sick. The work is too heavy for me. I want to resign and find a lighter job. The main Personnel Office told me that there are no rules for resignations. They asked me to go to a government hospital for an examination. They said they would grant me sick leave when my illness was certified by the hospital."

"You don't have to go for an examination anymore," he said. "After some consideration, the Bureau has decided to accept your resignation. Here is your certificate of resignation. You can go to the Accounting

Office to pick up your salary for the second half of December."

This was totally unexpected. At first, I thought I would face many difficulties. Now, it was all happening so smoothly. Immediately, I went to the Accounting Office and picked up my half month's salary of 60 Composite Units. As I walked out and approached the gate, the guards stopped me. They said that the Bureau was in a meeting and nobody was allowed to go in or out until it was over. They ordered me to wait. I returned to the Personnel Office to ask what was going on. They asked me to wait for the supervisor. After a few minutes, the supervisor came and told me that this delay was due to a misunderstanding. I was given permitted to leave. Since I was in a hurry to meet a relative for lunch, I did not bother to make further inquiries. As I walked out of the gate to take a tram, someone tapped me on my shoulder. When I turned around, I saw two men in uniform.

"What are you doing?" I asked.

"Come with me to the Police Station."

"What for?" I asked.

"You will know when we get there."

"I am busy today. I can't go. I'll go tomorrow."

"You must go. You are under arrest."

They showed me a warrant for my arrest. Under the case column, there were two big characters: fei te, "spy for insurgents". It felt as if a bolt of lightning had struck me.

When I got a hold of myself, I burst out, "No such thing. You people are acting recklessly making arrests for no reason at all. I am not going."

"You must go. We are acting on orders. Whatever you want to say, say it at the police station." Then one of them pointed a gun at me, and the other one handcuffed me. They forced me into an old black automobile.

They drove to the nearby police station. I was dragged out of the car and into a small room containing a table and a few chairs. I was pushed into one of the chairs. Several people came in with pen, ink, and paper, which they put in front of me, and said, "You know that the policy of the Party is 'leniency to those who confess openheartedly and mercilessness to those who do not.' Write out the organization you belong to, your position in it, the criminal acts you have committed, your goals, your plots, and your associates. Make a full disclosure. Otherwise, you will head down the road to extinction."

I was furious. I stood up and yelled, "I am definitely not an agent. I have nothing to confess. How can you abuse and oppress people like this?"

"You think this is oppression? You haven't seen anything yet. Be honest. Make a full confession."

"I am not going to write." I threw the paper and ink on the floor. One of the police slapped my face. I retaliated by punching him. Everyone circled around me. I resisted desperately with the few kung fu moves I had learned in my youth. The table and chairs fell over. Finally, I was subdued by several stronger men. I fell, hitting my head on the wall. I saw stars flashing and then lost consciousness. They took off my belt, loosened my shoestrings, and confiscated my watch and diary. Finally, I fell down senseless in the corner of the jail cell.

I was tenacious through the torture and abuse. I was neither dejected nor depressed. I thought that the only way to deal with such a disaster was to face it head-on. Little did I know how long the journey would be.

CHAPTER 2

IMPRISONMENT AND PRELIMINARY TRIALS

Chapter 2 *Imprisonment and Preliminary Trials*

BEGINNING OF THE ARREST

After many hours I woke up and looked around. The cell was about twenty square meters. Three sides were concrete walls. The fourth side was an iron barrier. Outside the barrier was a corridor, leading to a courtyard. A yellowish light in the corridor made the place even gloomier. Men lay crisscross in the cell with no space at all. My spot was in the corner next to the toilet bowl. There was no room to straighten my legs. The body odor and the stench of the toilet made me swoon. I sat against the wall and thought about what had happened to me.

After contemplating my situation, I realized that it was the culmination of the coercive forces I had endured for the last year and a half. Now they had used false charges to tear me down. Earlier on, I thought that a political entity, especially at the early stages of coming into power, would be concerned about law, order, and human rights. With due process, I would still have a chance to clear my name. Arrest and conviction must go through certain legal procedures and have some factual basis and proof. I knew that not only was I not an agent, but I had not even the slightest involvement with them. Except for December 19th, 1939, I had never taken part in any political activities. However inconceivable, I was now a political prisoner. This disaster made me realize that I did not truly understand the brutality of the Communists. My forthright disposition and hatred for pretense made me a target for attack. Under such wretched conditions, I hung onto the flimsy hope that justice would someday clear me and take me out of this cage. With just such thoughts, I sat amidst the stench in that dismal cell until dawn.

At the beginning of my detention, my foremost concern was for my elderly and feeble parents. My brother and I, with our limited income, had supported them. Now that I was locked up, the burden fell on my brother. My big worry was whether he could care for them in addition to supporting his wife and daughter.

I felt very weak and had no appetite. I still held on to the possibility that a trial might prove my innocence. Since no trial date had been set, I did not know what they were up to. I was anxious for a trial so that I could prove my innocence and wake up from this nightmare.

Days went by. One afternoon, while I was dozing, a guard called my name, saying that I was going to trial. Excitedly I jumped up and followed him through the courtyard, the corridors, and the stairs, entering the trial room. A cadre with Mao attire sat at a big table. He ordered me to sit across from him. Then two young fellows entered the room and sat silently against the wall. I didn't know whether they were guards or overseers.

The hearing was a question-and-answer session. In general, he inquired about my background, my reactionary past, the alleged anti-revolutionary organizations I had belonged to, my functions therein, and my activities that harmed the revolution and the citizens. Except for my background and my reactionary past, I could not answer any of the questions he asked. Not believing me, he kept up his interrogation and claimed that the government already had the evidence of my criminal past. What he wanted to find out was whether I was honest and forthcoming. He simultaneously enticed and threatened me with the Communist slogans "lenient to those who confess open-heartedly and merciless to those who refuse" and "refusal to confess is the road to extinction."

I protested, "How can you ask me to confess to something I have never done. The government always claims that it will verify the facts for their truthfulness. Why didn't you verify the facts of this case? You claimed that the government already has my criminal record. Where is it? Show it to me. If I committed the crimes, I will not deny it."

The squabble lasted for some time. Dusk came. The young men attending turned on the lights and the inquisition continued for a while longer. The interrogating officer realized that he could not force a deposition out of me. He gathered the stacks of documents and ordered the guard to escort me back to my cell. My fellow inmates had already had their meal. A portion had been saved for me. Agitated and distressed, I had no appetite. My cellmates asked me what I had just gone through. They were worried because the session had lasted so long. Tired, but not wanting to reject their goodwill, I gave them a sketchy report.

This hearing took place before the "Rules for the Punishment of Counterrevolutionaries" had been issued. The "Great Search and Arrest" and the "Great Repression" campaigns were also still to come.

LIFE IN JAIL

No trial was held for about two weeks. During this interlude, one of the inmates started bellowing in pain, waking the entire prison. At first, we had no idea what all the commotion was about, but then the person next to him found his shattered eyeglasses, and realized that he had swallowed the glass to kill himself. The guards immediately took him away by stretcher, presumably to the hospital. If he died before his case was settled, other would not be implicated.

In this case, the prosecutors and the warden were at fault. Before anyone is locked up, his glasses, belt, shoelaces, sharp objects, and any other possession that could be used for suicide are supposed to be confiscated. One of the inmates said that swallowing glass was the most painful way to die and one could not be saved from it. Dying with shards of glass cutting the stomach and intestine is slow and painful. We were horror-stricken by this incident.

The next day, the superintendent told us that the man who had swallowed the glass was a counterrevolutionary, a terrible criminal who had committed offenses and knew that the government would never let him go. He resorted to suicide to protect his organization and associates. The government had definitive proof of his criminal activities. If he had confessed open-heartedly and made accusations and disclosures to atone for his crime, he would have been treated with mercy. He did not have to resort to suicide. "You could learn a valuable lesson from this case."

I was also charged with being "an agent." As I witnessed the final blow to that fellow, I lamented his fate. I was in turmoil for a long time not knowing whether he lived or not. But from the tone of the warden, he died.

One day a foreigner was sent in. I talked with him in English and found out that he was a German Jew who had been persecuted and imprisoned by the Nazis. After release, he fled to England, married an English woman and became a British subject. After World War II, they came to Shanghai and established an international funeral home. The Communists shut it down because it was foreign-owned. All of his property was confiscated. He was arrested for returning to his business without permission.

"Your case is not serious. You will be released soon," I told him.

"Why are you here?" he asked.

"I was arrested because they think I am a counterrevolutionary spy."

After hearing my answer, he paused and said, "Your case is very serious. Recently, executions of counterrevolutionaries have been reported almost daily. From my experience with the Nazis, I can tell you that political persecutions are merciless."

What he told me was true. In the detention house, a designated inmate read the newspaper every day during our educational sessions. Afterward, we were required to discuss our impressions with the Superintendent. That's how I knew about the numerous break-ups of the rebels' cells and their executions. Knowing that this German was a medical doctor who knew a good deal about physiology, I asked him, "How painful is it to be shot?"

"Not too painful," he said. "You die before you've even heard the shot."

"Why is that? What is the explanation?" I asked with some doubt.

"The gun is aimed at your head. The sensation of pain comes from the cranial nerves. As the bullet destroys the brain tissue, the cranial nerves stop functioning. So you do not feel pain – as long as the shot is accurate and hits your head."

"What about being decapitated?" I asked.

"Beheading is painful, but it passes quickly because when the head is chopped off, all the blood drains away. A brain without blood does not function. When a bullet hits there is no muscle spasm. This is a sign that there is no pain." As a doctor, he had this knowledge. I felt relieved because it lessened my fear of executions.

Soon our conversation was noticed by the warden and he reported it to the superintendent, who called me in and asked what we talked about. I told him. He warned me that the rules forbade speaking in foreign languages. He ordered me not to talk to him in English and to submit a letter of repentance. Because he knew that the German Jew's minor offense was non-political and that we had not known each other beforehand, I was not punished. This was before the "Great Search and Arrest" and the "Great Repression" campaigns, before the rules became much stricter. The German Jew was soon released.

The delay of the trial depressed me. For the previous year and a half, through my contact with party members, cadres, and activists, I got to know the kind of people they were and how they behaved. In order to display loyalty to the Party and gain favor with their superiors, they disregarded the truth. To them, freedom of speech and freedom of thought were improper and unacceptable. The few who had some sense of justice and compassion were so intimidated that they did not dare reveal their true feelings.

Since my arrest on charges of being a "counterrevolutionary agent," none of my acquaintances, friends, or relatives dared to commiserate with me or defend me. If they had done so, they would have been implicated as sympathizers. Sympathizing with counterrevolutionary elements was a serious crime. That is why all the comrades, cadres, and activists totally aligned themselves with the Communist Party and authorities. According to the prevailing logic, if you were not a leftist, you must be on the right; if you were not a revolutionary, then you must be a counterrevolutionary. There was no middle ground. No one dared to speak up about justice and human rights.

There was no fair yardstick to measure the seriousness of a political offense. Prosecuting officers could sentence at will – setting any term of imprisonment or even the death penalty. I concluded that the accused were never acquitted. The prosecutors' motto was "arrest only, release never." Mistaken arrests, convictions, and excessive penalties were considered prudent, whereas lenient sentences were subject to scrutiny and criticism, and suggested a lack of revolutionary fervor.

The lockup was dark and gloomy, crowded and dingy, with little distinction between day and night. We could not tell how many days had passed. One day we suddenly heard firecrackers. This was a sign of Spring Festival—a new name for the lunar New Year. Not long before I was arrested, I told my parents that I would see them again at Spring Festival. Now I could not keep this promise. They might not even know I had been arrested. My absence and the lack of any information of my whereabouts would be devastating to them, yet there was no way I could send word to them. Since the war with the Japanese, my family had been strapped financially. Since the Communist take-over, conditions had deteriorated even further; my parents were now nearly destitute. Without my financial support, their ability to survive would be jeopardized.

At this time, the prison became even more crowded. Most of the new prisoners had been charged with counterrevolutionary offenses. Some of them had been arrested after they reported to the Registry for the

Members of Reactionary Parties and Organizations. The government had asked all members of the Nationalist Party, its outer circle of other political parties, the Sanminzhuyi Youth Corp, and the employees of the former government to register their former positions and to report any counterrevolutionary activities they had done.1 The government promised that if they registered and confessed open-heartedly, their burden of guilt would be relieved and they would not be prosecuted. However, those who did register were apprehended, on the basis that "the report was not truthful enough," "they shirked the important and left out the significant," or they were being "tricky and obscure." At the same time, the government proclaimed the "Rules for the Punishment of Counterrevolutionaries," followed by the "Great Search and Arrest" Campaign. They rounded up tens of thousands of "counterrevolutionaries" throughout Shanghai in a single night.

That was how the lockup became so crowded. The cell's toilet was far from sufficient for the group. People were dizzy from the smell. In the morning, after the wake-up bell, we had to wait in line to urinate and evacuate our bowels. When the bowl was full, it had to be emptied before we could resume. Many times, I became incontinent because of the unbearably long wait. Sleeping space was further constricted—shoulder touched shoulder, back against back. Our legs could never straighten out. It was worse than a pigsty. Food was bad from the very beginning and had gotten worse. The rice, soiled and undercooked, was hardly fit to swallow. I became thinner and thinner.

CHARGED WITH A CRIME

I longed for my second trial. Life or death, I wanted a timely settlement and an end to this misery. Many days passed and my anxiety mounted. One

---

1 Sanminzhuyi, in English the Three Principles of the People (Chinese: 三民主义; pinyin: sān mín zhǔ yì; also translated as San-min Doctrine) is a political philosophy developed by the founding father of the Nationalist Party of China (NPC), Sun Yat-sen. The three principles are often summarized as nationalism, democracy, and the livelihood of the people. This philosophy has been claimed as the cornerstone of the Republic of China's policy as carried by NPC.

day, around noon, an attendant summoned me. I saw this as my chance for change. Naturally, when one is in such a predicament, one will long for change. When I was escorted out of the cell, through the corridor, out of the gate, and into the courtyard, the brilliant sunlight took my breath away. The trees were budding and the birds were singing. I had been arrested a little before the Spring Festival; it was now early spring.

The trial had to take place in a sitting room. Because of the large number of cases, all the trial rooms were occupied. The prosecutor was the same one who had tried me before. Sitting next to him was a case reporter. Both appeared serious and cold. In addition to what the prosecutor had asked me before, he added some new and strange questions. Had I sent coded messages to Taiwan? Did I plan to join the remnant Nationalist forces to wage guerrilla warfare against the Liberation Army in the Taihu area?2 Had I persuaded the reactionary elements to form a group to start an anti-Communist and anti-government movement?

The trial was absurd but sinister with the death penalty looming as a possible outcome. Accusing someone of being an agent or spy was a most expedient charge. Even one's closest relatives and friends could not refute these charges since spying, by its nature, was a concealed activity.

Since I was on the edge of a dreaded fate, I decided to make a forceful defense. "You asked whether I sent coded messages to Taiwan. How can I communicate without a radio transmitter? I live in a dormitory with many people in the room. Where could I hide the transmitter? You also mentioned that I planned to join the remnant Nationalist Force for guerrilla warfare against the Liberation Army. Then I want to ask whether my previous charge of planning to go to Hong Kong to join the insurgents still stands. I have only one body. It is impossible for me to split myself in two and go on two different missions, one inside the country and one outside. My attempting to form an opposition group is even more unfounded. I have applied for an exit permit. How can I plan to form a group inside the country? Moreover, to form a group, one must first have associates. Who are my associates? Where are they? How can one person be considered a group?"

They had no reply to my rebuttal. After a long pause, the prosecutor

---

2 Taihu (Chinese: 太湖) is one of the largest freshwater lakes in the Yangtze Delta of China. Also known as Lake Tai or Lake Taihu, the lake lies in Jiangsu province and significant part of its southern shore forms its border with Zhejiang province.

spoke harshly, "You are the enemy of the people. There are no contradictions in our charges. You have done all these evil things. We have made you a sincere offer. Confess open-heartedly. The policy of the Communist Party is consistent—leniency for those who confess open-heartedly, no mercy for those who resist. Resistance is the road to death."

The word "death" was indeed threatening. Although I knew that my stubbornness was not in my own best interest, I was so enraged that I couldn't control myself. The inquisition continued. What followed were exchanges about my intention to join the Nationalists by way of Hong Kong and my listening to the false newscasts of the Voice of America. I repeatedly explained that I wanted to go to Hong Kong to work for the UNRRA, where my professor could get me a job.[3] The United Nations was a world peace organization, not a reactionary outfit. My wanting to go there could not be viewed as offering service to the enemy and therefore could not be treated as a crime. I only wanted to earn a living. I had no counterrevolutionary motives. Listening to the VOA and casually talking about their broadcasts was not a crime.

After my explanation, the officer spoke in an angry tone, "Then you are not guilty at all. You intellectuals are indeed crafty; you can rationalize anything. You want to take a flight to the United Nations. Where is the United Nations? Isn't it in New York? The United States is having a war with us in Korea. You want to go to America. Isn't that a way for you to give yourself to the enemy? You claim that listening to the Voice of America is not a crime. America is our enemy. The Voice of America is an enemy station, broadcasting rumors and information unfavorable to China. You not only listen to it but also spread their propaganda. You are not unaware of the damage caused by your activities, but instead you are pleased to be the enemy of the people, to overthrow the Communist government."

At the time of the "Resist U.S. Aggression and Aid Korea Expedition," conviction on any one of these accusations carried the death penalty.[4] Continued resistance would destroy my slim chance of escaping the death sentence. I was frightened and stopped arguing. I felt like a turtle in a jar;

---

3 UNRRA is the abbreviation for United Nations Relief and Rehabilitation Administration.
4 "Resist U.S. Aggression and Aid Korea Expedition", a slogan invented by the propaganda department of the Communist Party of China, went viral in mainland China during the Korean War.

there was no escape. The prosecutor had all the power. Self-defense and struggle were useless.

The trial took the whole afternoon. At the end of the trial, the prosecuting officer raised the stack of documents on the table and said to me, "You see, this is your entire file. The Party is meticulous in these matters. We have spared no resources in investigating you thoroughly. Your reactionary past and anti-revolutionary activities are all here with proof of times, places, witnesses, and materials. We can prove your guilt without your confession. What we want is to see whether you trust the Party, repent, confess voluntarily, and make disclosures—to strive for a more lenient disposition through introspection."

The prosecuting officer saw me with my head bowed and silent. He said to me, "Go back to your cell and mull it over. Make a complete and unreserved confession of your reactionary past and your counter-revolutionary activities. Then you will be free of guilt and receive a more lenient sentence. Okay, let's stop here. We will call you again in a few days." Then he had the guards escort me back to my cell.

The night was falling. Dinnertime had come and gone. The other inmates had saved me a bowl of rice with a few pieces of salty cabbage. Perplexed and disheartened, I had no taste for food. I had hoped for a speedy trial. I had thought a trial might clear up my problems. But now my problems were even more serious. The original charges were attempting to go to Hong Kong, listening to the Voice of America, making rumors, talking about the foreign reports on the Korean War, and making unfavorable remarks against the Communist Party and the Peoples' Government. At the trial, additional absurd allegations were added. It was clear that their goal was to exaggerate my crimes and punish me severely.

Defending myself was useless. While this was a matter of life and death to me, the same fate had befallen countless others. To the government and its administrators, I was but one of the thousands of routine cases. I came to realize that my situation was more intractable than I had realized. I became severely depressed and was agonizing over my situation as never before. This would be unimaginable for those who are from a democratic country with institutionalized protection of human rights.

STATION ROAD DETENTION HOUSE

Sleepless at night, idle during the day, and fearful day and night, I watched as my health deteriorated. There was a rapid turnover of detainees. Later, fewer detainees arrived since many were being sent directly to prison. This resulted in less overcrowding in the detention center. Although new arrivals moved out in a week or so, I had been in custody for almost two months, perhaps due to the complexity and seriousness of my case.

One gloomy rainy day, while I was dozing, an attendant called out, "Wake up. You are being transferred. Hurry and gather all your things. We will call you soon."

"Where am I being transferred to?" I asked.

"You will know when you get there."

Although I didn't know where I was going, I was glad to be saying goodbye to my miserable situation. An hour later I carried all my belongings—a wadded coverlet, a blanket, a porcelain enamel cup, a toothbrush, toothpaste, and so forth. They had confiscated my money and my college diplomas—one in English and one in Chinese—when I entered the detention center. These were not returned to me at this time. Altogether my worldly possessions weighed less than twenty pounds, but for someone as weak as I had become, this was a big load.

Handcuffed, I was loaded into a black police van. No other prisoners were being transferred, which was unusual. After the van was locked, I was engulfed in darkness. I likened myself to a sampan tossing about in the ocean and could only entrust my life to the waves and God.

After a long drive, the van stopped abruptly. When I emerged, I saw a vast yard, as wide as a football field. In the dark, I could not see much else. The guard escorted me to the far end of the yard where I saw an old-fashioned three-story wood and brick building. A number of security guards were at the gate. A corridor led to a big rectangular hall. The hall had a very high ceiling, encircled by the passageway outside the prison cells on the second and third floors. Looking up from the hall, I could see the passageway railings and cell doors. All doors, columns, and floors were painted a bright red, in sharp contrast with the white wall. Armed guards stood around the hall, at the stairs, and along the passageway—some with rifles, others with handguns, as if they were meeting an enemy brigade.

Chapter 2 *Imprisonment and Preliminary Trials*

I was led to a room near the stairway containing dozens of prisoners sitting on the floor. All their heads were bowed. The crowded room was eerily silent. A cadre led me to the end of the last row. With a stern and angry tone, he told me to bow my head and not look around. Then several more cadres came in with papers in hand.

First, they made roll call, then they announced, "Do you know where you are? This is the Station Street Detention House, district headquarter for counterrevolutionary criminals. All of you counterrevolutionaries have committed great crimes. You are the enemy of the people. You should know that the Communist Party and the Liberation Army have unparalleled strength. Your criminal activities will never escape the people's security network. Now that you have been arrested, you must lay bare all your sins as honestly as you can. Reproach yourself. Strive for more lenient punishment. The consistent policy of the government is lenient to those who confess open-heartedly, merciless to those who resist. Your crime is redeemable by serving your country. If you blindly refuse to change and continue to be an obstinate enemy of the people, you will head down the road to extinction."

It was the same old cliché I had heard so many times. After this sermon, we were led to the second floor and locked up. The cell was about twenty square meters, with red floors and doors, and white walls. There was a small opening on the wall, about eight feet from the floor, which served as a source of light and as a vent. Close to the ceiling on the left wall, there was a light that was shared with the next cell. There were about twenty of us, so we each had about one square meter, a bit roomier than the police lock-up. Our legs could stretch out when we slept. The cell's toilet was a big wooden barrel.

This place was called "Lock-up Headquarters for Counter-revolutionary Criminals." Communists did not use the term political prisoner, lest that elevated the status of the counterrevolutionaries. Most of these prisoners had been sentenced to life imprisonment or death. Only a few would survive, and then only after a term of hard labor. When a detainee was released for mistaken allegations, it was called "Release after Admonition." The Communists would never admit their mistakes.

This place had very strict rules that were complicated and all-encompassing. You were not allowed to whisper, not allowed to exchange information about cases with each other, and not allowed to exchange information about outside events, especially international affairs and the

Korean War. Nobody dared to break these rules. Insubordination could take you to the point of no return.

The main function of this prison was to verify the criminal activities of the detainees. They sent people out into the community to collect evidence. Within the prison, they used coercive methods to extort information from the prisoners. Their methods included haranguing, making threats, laying traps, and torture. Trials were held day and night. Sometimes calls were made in the middle of the night, catching people off-guard, making it more difficult for them to conceal testimony. Some of the captives were handcuffed and shackled. Nobody knew much about their cases since most of them received the death sentence.

Those who were literate, in addition to writing their own confessions, were required to write those of the less literate. I was one of these. Writing others' confessions was not an easy job because counterrevolutionaries' secret activities were usually convoluted and involved. To write for those from Fujian, Guangdong, Anhui and Yunnan was even more difficult because their Putonghua was very poor. 5 In order to please the administrators and gain favor with them, I helped in many cases. My eyes were red and swollen from writing till dusk with poor lighting. When I woke up in the morning, they were sealed shut with discharge.

At the Detention House, we took turns for certain chores. After having to empty the toilet barrel, the rest of the chores were minor. In order to hold the excrement of twenty people for a 24-hour period, the barrel had to be big and tall. The barrel was so tall that my legs dangled during defecation. Every morning, the barrel was nearly full. Lifting it was a lot of work. If my foot slipped and caused it to tip over, it would befoul others' bedding, clothing, and eating utensils that were on the floor. Fortunately, this was one disaster that I was spared.

During my stay at the Detention House, I was transferred once. From the time we got up to the time we retired, we were in an intensive reeducation program, interrupted only by our two meals. We had sessions on general information and the theoretical basis of the government's policies. Most of it was blared through loudspeakers. We read about the newly proclaimed laws and rules. The ideological struggle was a process of criticism and reprimand about the Four Undesirables and the rightists. We

---

5   Putonghua, or Pǔtōnghuà (普通话/普遍話), refers to the official spoken language of the People's Republic of China (PRC).

met either in large gatherings or small groups. The rest of the day was spent in trial or writing confessions. The goal was to speed up confessions, disclosures, and prosecutions so that judgments would be expedited.

Each cell was formed into a study group. Each group had a monitor who led the learning process and recorded the topics, confessions, disclosures, and prosecutions. Nobody knew the status of the monitor. He claimed he was a detainee just like us. But he never spoke about his case. He was trusted by the cadre and had a lot of authority. He ordered us about and treated us with contempt. He punished us. No one dared to contradict him. We suspected that he was a cadre in disguise, but no one dared ask.

There were some minor differences between the police lock-up and this one. The functions were the same—to extort testimonies and confessions—but this one was more terrifying. Day and night, we heard the clanking of shackles and the wails of sirens from vehicles transporting prisoners. It was said that the sirens signaled prisoners being taken to the Jiangwan Execution Ground.

One evening, a new detainee entered our cell. He was in his 20's, young and energetic. After a few days, we had gotten acquainted. I secretly asked him what his profession was and why he had been arrested. At first, he did not want to answer. Later, he bent his right index finger as a signal, but I could not figure out what that meant. I dared not press further because this type of communication was strictly prohibited. We whispered during the noisy moments—at meals, on arising, and before retiring. While we were eating, he confided to me that he was a member of the police corps that was stationed at the Jiangwan Execution Ground. He was one of the executioners. Then I understood what the bending of his finger meant. I asked him whether he had killed many people. He nodded and kept silent. I did not ask him why he was being detained because it would have required too long a conversation.

Our group monitor had once said, "For you people, there will be three ways to get out of this place. The first is the bicycle; that is the way home. The second is a black van; that is the way to prison. The third is a red truck; that is the way to the execution ground. You must trust the government. Make a thorough and open-hearted confession. Do your best to save yourself. Strive for the bicycle or at least the black van. You should never, never make yourself leave in the red truck."

From what the executioner revealed, I knew that the monitor's statement was not an idle threat. Since we heard the siren twice every morning, the number of executions was considerable.

THE VERDICT

I still had not had a formal trial at this prison. Many of the others were being tried almost every day. Some were called at midnight, when they were least able to mount a credible defense. This method was often used in complicated cases when the detainees refused to admit their guilt. My case was simple and did not involve any associates. That was apparently why they did not call me frequently.

With a faint hope of acquittal, I looked forward to my turn. After a long period of despair, I was finally called to trial. With a mixture of excitement and fear, I went to meet the challenge.

The trial took place in a small room. Aside from the prosecutor and myself, there was no one else. The questions he asked were almost identical to those at the police detention house. It was simply a replay. But his last question shocked me. He asked whether I had worked to form a counterrevolutionary organization.

Enraged, I countered, "How can you ask this kind of question without any evidence? Just what are your intentions?" He looked cold and oppressive.

Surprised at my retort, he replied sharply, "How do you know we don't have evidence? My questions are based on the evidence we have against you. We have all the evidence, and witnesses on when, where, what, and whom you talked to, and what you intended to do. Even if you don't admit your guilt, we already have everything we need to convict you. We are just giving you a chance to be honest, admit the facts, and repent. You can be punished without testimony."

I had never worked to form a counterrevolutionary organization, but how could I prove that? Under these conditions, any defense might make the situation even worse. The prosecutor saw that I wasn't reacting.

He continued, "You go back and think it over. Come to terms with yourself. I suggest that you write down a complete confession in the next three days. If you don't, you will regret it." The session was over; I was escorted back to my cell.

After being ordered to write a confession, I felt that my life had been turned upside down. I had trouble eating or sleeping. I developed a fever and an incapacitating headache. The three-day deadline passed with no confession. The monitor pressed me to write my confession. Seeing that I was sick, he gave me an extension. I took some traditional medicine and gradually improved over the next several days. After that, I was allowed a few more days of rest, excused from chores and reeducation sessions.

As I was recovering, the monitor ordered me to submit the confession in two days, with no more extensions. I felt very conflicted and reasoned that if I admitted that I intended to form a reactionary group, this (false) confession may have some palliative effect on my case. A criminal intention never acted on might be treated with leniency.

But on second thought, I should never falsely malign myself. If I admitted to something I had never done, I would be turning a trumped-up charge into a proven fact. I vaguely remembered from the learning material that the Communist Party was deeply and virulently against the opposition. They were demanding the suppression of reactionary groups at their earliest stages. If I did not make a categorical denial, my life might be at stake. Moreover, an admission of guilt would reward the person who had falsely implicated me. He would win more favor and continue to malign others, something I found intolerable.

Defying the oppressive tyranny, I made a forceful argument according to the facts. I told them that previous hearings established that I was guilty of planning to join the United Nations by way of Hong Kong. This I admitted to. Now, I was being charged with the intention of working for a counterrevolutionary organization. The former was my wanting to leave the country. The latter was my engaging in anti-government activities that required me to remain in the country. It was impossible for me to be in both places simultaneously. The two charges were contradictory. I finished writing my "non-confession" and submitted it. Contrary to what I had hoped, I was not called again for a long time. Meanwhile, I was very worried that my "non-confession" might bring me further misfortune.

One afternoon, a security officer came and took me through the large prison, finally reaching a row of cottages. I was escorted inside where the prosecutor and court reporter were sitting at a table. About four meters away, I sat facing the table and handcuffed to the chair. The hearing began by my stating my name, age, domicile of origin, and the criminal activities I was charged with. I responded according to the facts, acknowledging what I had done, and denying categorically what I had not done. As to the criminal activities, I presented only the facts without conceding the criminal nature of the acts. Curiously, the prosecutor did not respond to my denials but asked for the facts and motives of each event in great detail.

The question-and-answer session went on for over two hours. Evening was coming. The prosecutor seemed ready to end the session. But then he continued with a few more questions. Some of them had no bearing on the case, such as, "On such and such a day, you took a stroll with so-and-so at Wusong Estuary. What was that for?"

At the end of the trial, the prosecutor released me from the chair, asked me to read what was recorded, and to put my fingerprint on it. The record was seven or eight pages long. The first two pages consisted of my name, age, domicile, family background, education, profession, etc. The rest was in a question-and-answer form. There were many omissions. Some of the answers were left completely blank.

After looking it over, I asked, "The record is not even complete and you want me to put my fingerprint on it?"

The two of them looked at each other and did not answer. I read through the rest and did not find any problems. The reporter was a poorly educated teenager without sufficient education to be functioning as a court reporter. It would not make any difference if the record were complete or not. To fill in those omissions would require another round of verbal contention. Weak and tired, already on the brink of collapse, I resigned myself to letting them fill in the blanks any way they liked. I quickly put my fingerprint under my name and in between the connecting pages.

Since I was in the right, I felt confident. I asked, "Do you have any more questions? Ask me now so you don't have to call me again."

He replied, "Right now there are none. You can go back." I thought this would be my last trial, and with that comforting thought, I returned to my cell.

Chapter 2 *Imprisonment and Preliminary Trials*

THE RED POLICE TRUCK

The weather got warmer, but we were not allowed to bathe. The body odor had escalated to epic proportions. There were no calendars or newspapers in the jail. I did not know how many days went by. One day after lunch, a security officer called my name and number. The officer asked me to get my belongings ready because a transfer was imminent.

I became apprehensive because we detainees believed that transfers signified a danger to one's life. My fellow inmates saw that I was in a daze and urged me to hurry up and get my things together. The prisoners, all suffering together, empathized with each other. They helped me to pack my bedroll and tie up my belongings. They also put some soap and toilet paper in my bundle. As soon as this was done, the security officer came to take me. With difficulty, I carried the bedroll on my back and the other belongings in my hands.

As I walked out, I turned around and said, "See you again." They answered with the same. What a hollow goodbye since we knew we were unlikely to ever see each other again.

I was led to a big hall where more than one hundred inmates were sitting in straight lines. Everyone had his head bowed; no one was talking; none of them took notice of me. I was ordered to sit at the end of the line. When I looked up, I saw armed guards on the second floor closely watching the inmates below. At the front end of the hall, I saw a long table with packages of various sizes and shapes. Cadres were calling the names of the inmates to pick up the packages. After I picked mine up, I realized it contained the items confiscated during my first arrest—my watch and some money. The return of my possessions comforted me. Maybe there was a chance I'd be going home, but judging from the serious atmosphere, that was unlikely.

From one of the packages, a cadre took out a cigarette lighter and asked another cadre, "Can we return this to him?"

"No," the other replied, "we shall make another list and hand it over to them."

From this exchange, it was clear that we were not being released but merely being handed over to another institution.

After the packages were returned, the chief cadre ordered all of us to stand up in pairs, to be chained together by shackles. It became even more difficult to carry our things. Lined up in columns of four, we shuffled out of the gate. Many motorcycles, jeeps, and a single red truck were in the courtyard. With the guards pointing their swords at us, we boarded the red truck. I remembered with terror the words of the monitor, "You should never, never get on the red truck. That is the vehicle that takes you to the execution ground." I asked myself, "Am I going to be executed?"

Looking back on my life, I knew that I had never done anything malicious or tried to benefit myself at somebody else's expense. I was an ethical, law-abiding human being. I had never been a member of any political party, never engaged in any political activity. How could my life be extinguished in the name of a political crime? I was filled with sadness. Ever since my arrest, the possibility of being executed had been on my mind. For my parents, the death of their son would be devastating. For me, the thought of my own demise no longer seemed all that terrible.

After we boarded the red truck, the door was locked. It was so dark I could not see a thing. After a while, with the light seeping through the seams of the back door, I could see a few shadows. I took out the watch that had just been returned to me and wound it. I set the hands on 12 so that I could measure the length of our trip. I figured that if the ride took over thirty minutes we were most likely headed for the execution ground at Jiangwan.

After twenty minutes, the truck went up an incline and came down again. That was a bridge that had to be passed on the way to Jiangwan. But suddenly the van stopped and I heard the opening of an iron gate. I knew that the execution ground would not be this close and that it had no iron gates!   The more experienced inmates said, "This is Tilanqiao Prison."

CHAPTER 3

TILANQIAO PRISON

GUNSHOTS OUTSIDE THE WINDOW

The atmosphere of the prison was quite different from that of the detention house. In the detention house, armed guards were everywhere; at the prison, they were seldom seen. The officers of the detention house treated the inmates harshly and enforced the rules strictly; the jailers of the prison were much more relaxed with the inmates. They did not bother you if you looked around or talked softly. On the other hand, the security measures were quite thorough. The prison was encircled by a thick wall, over five meters high, with electrified barbed wire on top. The jail was a 7-story concrete building with doors made of iron bars. The door locks had to be turned three times to open so that incidents in one part of the prison would not spread to another.

The entire prison was made of innumerable small concrete cubicles, about 2 x 1½ meters. In the corner sat a wooden toilet bowl. The rule was that all bedding had to be meticulously folded up in the opposite corner. Two prisoners had to sit huddled on one side of the cell, leaving the other half for the third person to walk about. I felt like a caged animal. Having three people to a cell was barely tolerable, but after a while a fourth person came in. And later, when the weather turned warm, a fifth person. At night, we slept two on one end and three on the other, flesh against flesh, head against feet.

According to a new inmate, the reason the prison became so crowded was that the Communists had rounded up many counterrevolutionary suspects throughout Shanghai one night in what was called the "Great Search and Arrest." All police lock-ups were at full capacity. Many suspects were sent directly to prison. As a rule, black vans were used for transferring inmates from one prison to another, while red ones delivered prisoners to the execution ground. But because of the sudden increase in prisoners, the red trucks were added for regular transport.

All day long the prison loudspeakers broadcast the policies of the Communist Party, new developments in domestic and international affairs, the rules and precepts that inmates had to observe, and grandiose assurances of combining leniency with strictness in assessing penalties. Meanwhile, the pressure for confession slackened. Even though my case was still pending, I felt a bit more relaxed.

As the weather got warmer, five inmates occupying three square meters became intolerable. I developed a severe rash. The administration gave me a folk remedy, which proved ineffective. Fortunately, during the next round of placement, I was transferred to the basement. Although damp and dark, it was cooler and I gradually got better. In order to avoid conspiracy through prolonged contact, the administration periodically rearranged the cellmates. This gave me ample opportunity to meet people from different walks of life and hear all sorts of news. Because some of the prisoners had been seized recently, I was able to learn about the "Great Search and Arrest" and the "Great Repression." Since my case was still pending, these stories terrified me.

During one of the reshufflings, I was placed in a cell on the west side of the building. Ominous sharp bursts of sound intruded our mornings like an uninvited guest. We tried to convince ourselves that it was merely noise coming from the nearby factories, but we suspected that it was gunfire. But since the prison was in a busy section of the city, there did not seem to be any reason to fire guns. However, since the bursts came at the same time each morning, they could not be accidental.

During the next round of reshuffling, I was moved to the top floor, also to a cell with windows facing the west. Right after I moved in, a worker covered the window with a lime solution. This aroused my concern. Why were they obscuring my view? Because of the hot weather, the windows were temporarily left open.

The next day, at about ten in the morning, a worker came and shut the windows. The room rapidly became stifling. As we were eating breakfast, we suddenly heard what sounded like a bolt of thunder. Clearly, this was a machine gun. Frightened, I dropped my box of food. The mystery of the sounds and the window covering was now clear. Half an hour later, the worker opened the window. After a while, we understood the pattern. Prisoners, handcuffed and escorted by four armed guards, were taken onto the prison grounds and shot each morning. Those who were not taken joked, "We can look forward to two more aluminum boxes," – two more meals, and perhaps tomorrow would be their turn to be executed.

As the days went by, the punctual gunfire quieted down. We hoped that the "Great Search and Arrest" and the "Great Repression" might be coming to an end. But that proved to be wishful thinking.

As a rule, executions were not done on the grounds of the prison. After the "Great Search and Arrest", so many were sentenced to death that neither the execution ground nor vehicles could handle the load. So the west yard was used as a temporary execution ground. According to the new arrivals, the nearby residents had complained about the executions, which both adults and children could witness from the upper floors of their housing. The authorities, therefore, ceased on-site executions and went back to the old system of transporting—via the red truck—those marked for death.

PRISON UPROAR

About the same time, I experienced something new and strange—the prisoners' sleep uproar. One night, I dreamt that I was in jail, with a crackling fire trying to consume me. I desperately shook the iron bars of the cell and yelled to get out. When I woke up, I found myself doing exactly what I dreamt. All the other inmates were doing the same thing. Their yelling was as loud as thunder, but it was short-lived. The uproar turned into a dead silence when the warden warned everyone to lie down and be quiet; whoever yelled again would be severely punished.

The next day at noon, a special assembly was called due to the sleep uproar incident. The warden said that counterrevolutionaries had instigated the sleep uproar the night before. Their purpose had been to incite a riot. The warden ordered the prisoners to find out who had initiated the sleep uproar in each cell. He asked the initiators to identify themselves so as to be leniently punished, and for those who knew the instigators to disclose it in order to be rewarded for meritorious service. He required everyone to make clear what state of mind he was in at the time of the sleep uproar.

Nobody could say for sure who had started the yelling. As to each individual's state of mind, this was also a thing that could hardly be defined. So in the end we made very sketchy reports, hoping to muddle through.

About a week later, the loudspeaker announced that the sleep uproar had been instigated by counterrevolutionaries in an attempt to incite a prison riot. After a thorough investigation, three principal offenders were identified and convicted. We were warned that all prisoners must act with restraint and conform to the rules; the wicked would not go unpunished. After hearing this announcement, we all knew the case was closed. How those three people had been identified and whether they had been given a fair trial were not the kind of things we cared about. All we cared about was our own existence. We were numb to the misfortunes of our fellow prisoners.

The accusation that counterrevolutionaries instigated the sleep uproar was fabricated. Subsequently, I learned from psychology books that sleep uproar in prisons or military camps was a sign of hysteria and a manifestation of underlying anxiety when people have to live in close quarters. Sleep uproar in military camps was especially terrifying, as the soldiers would oftentimes open fire in their sleep. This sleep uproar occurred in a prison in which each cell housed only three to five prisoners. Thus, a large disruptive riot was not feasible. Even if the uproar had been instigated, there was no chance of it turning into a riot. Even so, those convicted of instigating the sleep roar could never hope to receive a merciful disposition.

THE SENTENCE

The sentence that I had long awaited finally came. With fear and relief, I received the most important disposition of my life. Fearful, because I knew the judgment would not be fair. Relief, because for better or worse, the prolonged uncertainty would finally be swept away. If I were sentenced to death, it would be an unbearable blow to my family. The German Jewish doctor had told me that execution at gunpoint was not painful, but could I be sure he was telling the truth? Maybe he told me that just to ease my fears.

It was noon on a warm day. The brilliant summer sun shone through the window into my cell, where I was lying in a corner. A guard called my name and number. Heart palpitating, I immediately sensed that something important was about to happen. At the same time, another inmate in my cell was called also. The two of us, barefoot and with sleeveless shirts, were led to a wide corridor on the ground floor

There were already one hundred or so inmates sitting on the ground in rows. The judgment session had already begun. Whoever was called was led to the end of the corridor. I could not see what was happening there. Each case took about two minutes.

I was called after about ten cases. A guard led me to the end of the corridor and then into the entrance hall, where a temporary office had been set up. A few cadres sat around a table, upon which was a stack of files. I was ordered to stand three meters away from the table. The officer in the center shouted for me to drop my hands and bow my head. After verifying my name, age, and domicile, a judgment was read, "So and so, having worked under the reactionary clique before Liberation, participated in some adverse services. After the Liberation, through the magnanimous policy of the government, he was retained to serve. But because of his obstinacy, he did not reform or showed any remorse, and continued to be the enemy of the people. He listened to the Voice of America, spread untruthful rumors, attempted to muster reactionary forces, and schemed to join opposition forces through Hong Kong. It is ordered that so and so be sentenced to a 12-year term of servitude. No judgment paper will be given. Appeals will not be permitted. (signed) The Commander of the Liberation Army of the Shanghai District."

Afterward, my cellmate and I were escorted back to our cell. He received a 15-year sentence for being in the Nationalist army. Later we found out that everyone in that session received prison sentences; no one was sentenced to death. Death sentences were passed out early in the morning and carried out immediately.

A 12-year sentence. At least, my life was spared. But how could I bear such a long imprisonment? For the last two years, I was still a citizen, even though I had endured bitter hardship. Now that I am convicted, how would I live through the following days and years?

A few days later, the sentenced prisoners were brought together to listen to an announcement. "Your reduced sentences are evidence of the government's big-hearted policy. You should acknowledge your guilt, obey the law, and be grateful to the government. Change your life philosophy; eradicate all of your previous faults, repent, and start your life anew. You should understand that your judgment is not unalterable. Some of you have committed crimes that have not been reported and are yet to be discovered. Confess without reservation and you could win a more lenient disposition. The government has gotten hold of all your materials. This is your last chance to confess completely and start your new life. Do not hesitate."

Shortly after the sentencing, there was another round of reshuffling. I was moved to a cell for four. Three sat against one wall, leaving half of the cell for the fourth prisoner to pace along the other wall. It was late fall and a chill was in the air. Wadded coverlets provided a little warmth at night.

One day, at a learning session, the loudspeaker announced:

"You, the criminals, have injured the nation and the people. You are the enemies of the people. Your many faults are deeply rooted. The people are rightfully angry with you. You deserve to be punished even more severely. But because the generous policy of the Party is to heal the sick and rescue the drowning, you have been given limited terms of servitude. You have an opportunity to give up your evil ways and start your life anew. Now, an even better opportunity is on the way. The government is ready to be lenient by sending you to *laogai* 'reform through labor.' It will allow you to undertake constructive activities in an organized and disciplined environment. You will acquire useful skills and habits so that you can earn a living. This reeducation and rectification will be a new chapter in your life. It will change your life philosophy and worldview from 'getting something for nothing' to 'living by your own efforts.' Renounce your reactionary viewpoint. Align with the Party and government, and become a new person. This great 'reform through labor' policy is an innovation, unlike any other, of the Party and government, a practical actualization of revolutionary humanitarianism. You should never again commit sabotage. You should never again commit counterrevolutionary misdeeds. Repeat offenders will be dealt with severely. The People's judicial network is omniscient and boundless. Do not think you can misbehave undetected."

We were excited about leaving this prison and start our labor assignment. Working would at least give us the freedom to move about. But we didn't really know what "reform through labor" was. In response to this announcement, I compared myself to a small boat on the high sea, facing stormy winds and waves. The boat could turn over at any time, but there was still the chance of rescue. The judicial system of Communist China, when it first came into power, initiated three harsh practices: 1) the reform through labor program, 2) trial of nonmilitary cases by military courts, and 3) capital punishment. There was no independent judicial system; the courts were merely the instrument for implementing government policies.

RE-SENTENCING

One day at noon the warden came, asking me and another man to follow him. We were led down the same old corridor. Already some one hundred people were on the floor, very much like the day when judgments were given. Astonished and apprehensive, I asked the person next to me what was going on. He said he didn't know, but possibly it was re-sentencing. I was not convinced of this, since the judgments had been given only a few days ago. How could there be re-sentencing when no new events had occurred during this period?

When the roll call began, I was one of the first ones to be called. It was a repeat performance of the other day. I was ordered to drop my hands and bow my head. But for a few minutes the new sentence was not announced. The officers flipped some papers in my file and whispered to each other. In the end, one of them ordered me to go back and wait. I was taken back to my original place at the end of the hall.

The re-sentencing went on. With an average of two minutes for each person, it took almost four hours to complete the cases. Those four hours were hard to endure. I waited anxiously on the concrete floor, barefoot and wearing few clothes, shivering as the sun went down. When I was at last called, the entire hall was empty.

By the time my new sentence was given, the officer was exhausted. He mumbled the new judgment rather quickly. New text had been added to my sentence—"Affronting the government and threatening the public"—but my 12-year term of forced labor was not lengthened.

After the "new" sentence, I was taken back to my cell. I took only a few bites of my supper, leaving the rest for the other inmates. The other man who had gone with me had already returned. His situation was the same; while the wording had changed, the sentence was unaltered.

According to him, re-sentencing was dangerous. Judgments handed down to counterrevolutionaries during the civil war and the early years of the People's Republic were relatively light. With re-sentencing, most of the light sentences were escalated to life sentences and some to the death penalty.

How he came to know such details, I did not ask. He had been a civilian officer of the Nationalist military, a college graduate, and knew English. Subsequent events proved that he was right. A handsome twenty-year-old prisoner, who had received a written judgment, was transferred to our cell. Since none of us had received written judgments, we were curious and asked to see his paper. His written judgment was a joint sentence with his six associates. As armed secret service agents from Taiwan, the other six were seized when trying to slip into the mainland through the Zhoushan archipelago of Zhejiang province. The principal culprit was a young girl, whose offence was literally seducing men to join counterrevolutionary activities. This young man was not one of them but had helped them hide the ammunition. When they were first sentenced, everyone was sentenced to a term of forced labor. He received a three-year term. At re-sentencing, the other six were given the death penalty. His term was increased to ten years of labor. At the executions, he was sent to witness their deaths. The girl, not even twenty, was beautiful, intelligent, well-versed in song and music, and a good dancer. As a member of a troupe, she frequently performed in the theatre. Right before the execution, while blindfolded, she smiled at her associates.

From this example, we realized that re-sentencing was perilous. But our penalties had not changed, so what was the re-sentencing for?

CHAPTER 4

FIXING THE HUAI RIVER IN NORTHERN ANHUI

Chapter 4 *Fixing the Huai River in Northern Anhui*

THROWN INTO REFORM THROUGH LABOR

After the re-sentencing, everything seemed more settled. Every day, a certain number of prisoners were sent to the rooftop for exercise and fresh air. The rooftop was about 15 X 50 meters, which seemed vast after my long confinement in a tiny cell. The wall was three meters high, topped with electrified barbed wire. At one end, above the wall, was a watch post from which the guard overlooked our activities. We got to stay on the roof for thirty minutes each time. Some prisoners had become too weak to walk. After a few sessions on the roof, they started to regain their strength and appetite. Healthy prisoners would become better laborers.

During this period, the warden lectured us over the loudspeaker, encouraging us to work energetically for the reform through labor program in order to earn more generous treatment from the government. He said that enthusiastic participation could shorten our sentences. I had heard that prisoners with long sentences were often released before their terms were up, especially if their crimes had been political. Thus, all of us thought that vigorous participation in the reform through labor program could lead to early release.

At one of the learning sessions, we were told that we were permitted to write to our immediate family asking for daily necessities, such as clothing. This unexpected good news brought us joy but not for long. A so-called writer was to fill in the quantity next to the item listed on a mimeographed form. We were not allowed to write the letters ourselves. Obviously, they were afraid we would use codes to communicate with the outside world. The Communists took great precautions against us, "the people's enemy."

I had no immediate family in Shanghai. My parents in my hometown had long been in dire straits. I definitely could not write them for help, but subsequently, I thought perhaps my brother was still in Shanghai. I wrote to him, so that he could comfort my parents with the news that I was still alive. For a long time there was no response, so I thought that the letter must have been lost or never sent.

But finally I received a package of shirts, tank tops, and socks. My name and assigned number was written handsomely on the package, in what appeared to be the handwriting of a lady. But as stated in the rules, there was no sender's name. I turned over and over in my mind all the acquaintances who might have sent me this package but could not think of who the person might be. At that time, to send a package to an inmate, one had to wait in line at the gate for five to six hours. She could also be implicated by associating with a convict. Whoever it was, I would be grateful to her for the rest of my life. I carefully preserved the cloth that the package was wrapped in. I kept it with me until it was eventually stolen in the labor camp.

The weather became cooler and the leaves turned yellow. Our bare feet needed socks. We all needed more clothes. One day, after supper, an announcement came through the loudspeaker, "Those who are in the reform through labor program are good prisoners who confessed openheartedly. Your cases have been rigorously investigated. You are very fortunate to have this opportunity. You criminals should, from the bottom of your heart, admit your faults, obey the law, and be grateful to the government. Be content with the reform process. Work hard and study diligently. Radically change your life philosophy and worldview. Turn over a new leaf and become a new man. Now, the list is finalized and the arrangements are made. The following is a list of the squadrons, brigades, and battalions each of you belongs to. Listen carefully." What followed was a long list read out by several announcers. Over a thousand people formed the two battalions. Each battalion was divided into brigades, and the brigades into squadrons.

A few days later, after the evening meal, everybody was ordered to pack his belongings and prepare for departure. We would start our journey that very night. The long-anticipated end of imprisonment was now at hand. Packing was quick and easy because we only had few possessions. We were given some long strips of cloth for our backpacks. The superintendent announced that everybody could only bring twenty kilos; anything over that would have to be left behind. Those who hated parting with what they had tried to pack as tightly as possible, so that their backpacks might look slimmer. In fact, the packs were not weighed. What I had was simple—one silk bedding coverlet, one felt blanket, a few pairs of underwear, and some socks. Everything fit into a small pack except for some utensils, towels and a toothbrush, which I planned to carry in a cloth bag. The weather was very cold, so I was wearing most of my clothes. I felt envious because some had more than me. But in the end, I got through the journey much easier with the lighter load.

After two hours of hurried preparation, I heard the loudspeaker issue more rules, more minutia. An hour later came the order to leave. Everyone put on his backpack. Those who had the heavy ones needed help getting them on. Fortunately, we were not handcuffed this time. The entire assembly was divided into two columns as we walked out the gate.

Many police trucks were waiting. We proceeded in an orderly fashion and boarded the trucks. It was midnight and raining. The trucks were fully loaded and locked. It was pitch black inside. All of us were whispering about why we started off so late at night. Contrary to our expectation that we would stop at the local train station, the trucks kept going until reaching the train station in a neighboring town. At the dimly lit platform, roll call was made before we boarded the enclosed freight cars. Each freight car could house three squadrons of twenty each. The freight cars had small holes for ventilation, located at the four upper corners. As daylight seeped in, we could vaguely identify one another. In the center was a big wooden barrel emitting its signature odor.

It was dawn by the time we all settled in. Exhausted from the past twenty-four hours, we used our backpacks as pillows and lay down with our clothes on. Even though there was no room to stretch out and mud all over the floor, everyone fell asleep quickly.

I woke up with the train still thundering forward. The high beam of sunshine through the vent hinted that it was already noon. After a while, the train stopped. The door of the boxcar opened. The brilliant sun and the fresh air rejuvenated the dark and soiled boxcar. Breathing clean air was quite refreshing. After a night of sleeping in the fetal position, moving around and stretching felt good. Soon the officer called those prisoners who were assigned as heads of the squads to meet on the platform. When the heads returned, they ordered us to empty our bladders and bowels, and then empty the barrels; after which we would eat lunch. The squads went out of the boxcars in an orderly fashion to the platform to eat a meal of coarse rice, salted radish, and plain water. The radish smelled strongly of fish. It had been made in salt water leftover from salting fish. It was so unappetizing that I couldn't finish it.

The journey resumed after our meal. The train moved slowly, for a while stopping at every station. Not until the third afternoon did we get off the train. We had reached our destination but had not been told its name. After we got off the train, we walked for a considerable time on a bumpy dirt road, eventually reaching the shore of a wide river.

I saw a long row of boats on the river. These boats were not equipped with motors and did not use oars or poles but, instead, were linked together and pulled by a steamboat. After we boarded these boats, we were given two corn buns and some salted radish but no water. The radish made us very thirsty. The clever prisoners tied their enamel cups to a shoestring to take water from the river to drink. I was lucky enough to drink one cup. It tasted as good as morning dew.

The boats set off at dusk. All the windows were covered so that we could not see where we were going. We sat against one another on wooden benches and fell asleep. The boats anchored before dawn the next morning. We staggered ashore and walked twenty kilometers to the town of Shuanggou, in Sihong County of Jiangsu Province. After a brief pause, we walked a few more kilometres to our final destination, the closest point between the Huai River and Hongze Lake.[1]

---

[1] Hongze Lake (simplified Chinese: 洪泽湖; traditional Chinese: 洪澤湖; pinyin: Hóngzé Hú) is the fourth largest freshwater lake in Jiangsu Province of China. A major part of the Huai River pools into the Hongze Lake. The Huai River (Chinese: 淮河; pinyin: Huái Hé) is located midway between the Yellow River and Yangtze River, the two longest rivers and largest drainage basins in China. The Huai River, notoriously vulnerable to flooding, has historically changed its river course for multiple times. During the Sino-Japanese War, the Chinese army, in an attempt to block the Japanese southward advance through the North China Plain, blew up the dikes of the Yellow River near Zhengzhou, flooding a vast area in Henan province. The flood in 1938 has greatly disrupted the Huai River system. After World War II, extensive work to control the flood of Huai took place. In the early 1950s, the headwaters of the Huai and its western tributaries were controlled by constructing many large retention dams. In 1957 a second stage of flood control began on the southern tributaries. After 1958 the area south of the Huai was incorporated into a large coordinated irrigation system.

Chapter 4 *Fixing the Huai River in Northern Anhui*

EXCAVATION WORK AT THE HUAI RIVER

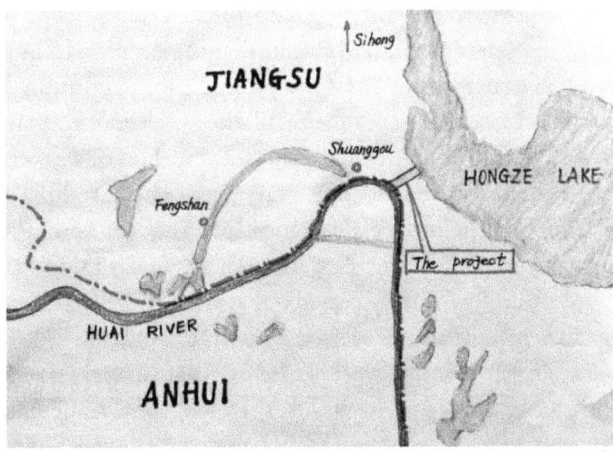

The two bodies of water were separated by a highland less than ten kilometers long. Our task was to dig a canal to link them up. The highland was about 25 meters above the ground. Since they wanted the canal to be 25 meters deep, we would need to dig a total of fifty meters. Although the riverbed was only about fifty meters wide, because of the depth required, the open end had to be 200 meters wide. The purpose of the project was to channel the overflow of the Huai River into Poyang Lake, thus preventing flooding. For that reason, the channel had to be finished before the rainy season. The total number of reform laborers mobilized for this project was well over ten thousand.

Our campground was two kilometers from the work area. We made A-shaped shelters from rushes. The sleeping space allotted to each laborer was thirty centimeters wide and eighty centimeters long. It was so cramped that adjacent prisoners had to sleep head-to-foot. If one were not totally exhausted, one could not fall asleep. The food was so bad that if one were not famished, one could hardly swallow it.

The ten thousand-plus laborers undergoing reform had arrived from all over the country. Our battalion of more than a thousand was responsible for one hundred meters of the project. We worked in two shifts - one from noon to midnight, the other from midnight to noon. Meals were served at 6 in the morning and 6 in the evening. The rest of the time we worked non-stop to get this project done before the flooding season.

The job consisted of scooping out the earth and transporting it away from the site. The work began from the top of the hill. Not only was the earth dry and porous, but moving the dirt from the top down was relatively easy. But after a while, when the digging deepened, the dumping area had to be farther away. The task became more and more difficult, especially after rain, which made the dirt heavy and slippery. Portage with wheelbarrows became extremely laborious. Even though we were already stretched to the limit, the brigadier generals of the battalion and their supervisors thought the progress was too slow, that we were not putting out our best effort. When they saw the porters and the pushers of the wheelbarrows walk slowly, they lashed out at them angrily and sometimes even flogged them, like scenes of slave ships in the movies.

In fact, reform laborers were worse off than slaves. Slaves were the property of the slave owners, to whom they had some undeniable value. Reform laborers were the enemies of the people, the dregs of society. They were used as long as they had some utility. Otherwise, they would be extinguished. We had no choice but to continue this inhumane assignment. Our ultimate goal was an early release. The reform through labor officers had repeatedly declared that the government would reassess the penalty of each individual in accordance with his performance, his loyalty to the government, his guilty conscience, and his obedience to the law. Posters such as "Commutations in May," "Reward for Good Workers," "Align with the Government," and "Strive for a More Lenient Disposition" were all over the fields. In addition, the loudspeakers were broadcasting high-pitched revolutionary songs in order to incite more work out of the prisoners. As one of the officers said, "Your labor must be burning with ardor."

With these enticements, the prisoners endured great pains to give off themselves completely. The cadres said, "The project must be completed before the rainy season; otherwise, the deluge of rain will make the work even more difficult."

Everybody wanted to see the project completed ahead of schedule, so they could say goodbye to this miserable life. We urged each other on to work harder. The "exhibitionists" worked harder when they saw cadres around. To make a more favorable impression, they would loudly encourage others to work harder.

As the work went on, the weather got warmer and the bed of the canal got deeper. By mid-June, it was already over ten meters deep. Then disaster hit. The canal caved in. It was a little before midnight, close to the changing of shifts.

I had just dumped some dirt out of the wheelbarrow and was pushing it to the canal bed. Suddenly, there was a big boom followed by a rumbling noise. As I looked up, I saw a wreath of dark smoke rise from the canal bed. A lot of dirt and rocks had fallen down. A sharp stone rolled onto my bare feet, making a small cut. The whole area became murky from the flying dust. After a while, I could not see anything, but I could hear plaintive cries for help.

After a while, a few cadres and soldiers from the Liberation Army came to the scene with lanterns. Under the faint light, they used shovels to dig out those buried in the debris. The only ones that could be saved were those at the edge of the site whose clothes and body parts were exposed. During the cave-in, huge rocks had fallen from a great height. A large number of prisoners were buried alive in this disaster. I moved rocks with my bare hands and carried the injured or dead to shore. I was horrified to see one of them with blood gushing out of multiple orifices. One of his legs was broken, with the bone sticking out.

The next morning, the commander of the battalion gave a speech in which he touched lightly upon the disaster. He said the cave-in occurred because the holes were dug at an angle. No mention was made of the number of casualties, nor did he caution not to dig at an angle in the future. The holes were dug at an angle so that the upper part would fall down by gravity, saving a lot of labor. In order to work faster and more efficiently, digging at an angle had become standard practice. Normally, digging a hole at an angle was carried out to a moderate depth, so that when the upper part fell, the probability of a landslide was minimal. This time, they had dug too far and too deep. The upper part was a colossal twenty meters from the bottom. The supervisors were reluctant to prohibit this practice because they wanted to see the work progress faster. The safety of the hard-working prisoners was never on their minds.

It was now mid-summer and very hot. I was on the second shift this time—the shift from midnight to noon. One night, about two hours after we reported for work, a strong chilly wind blew in from the northwest, an unusual phenomenon in the summer. The wind gained force and became even colder, followed by lightning and pouring rain. Water from the shore flowed from the slopes into the trench we had been digging for months. The water level rose quickly. At first, I took shelter on a mound of earth in the trench and held a basket over my head to ward off the rain. When the water level reached my waist, I tried to get ashore. But the water-soaked clay was very slippery. After a few steps on the slope, I slipped back into the water. I saw many of my fellow prisoners trying to get out of the canal like a swarm of ants. Seeing a terraced slope nearby, I swam toward it and tried to get ashore from there. I had to stick my hands deep into the clay in order to climb out. When I reached the shore, my body was completely covered in clay.

Under the dim light of the work site, I walked precariously on the slippery road toward the shelters. As I slowly walked from the light into complete darkness, the roar of the thunder and rain masked any human sounds. I lost my sense of direction and became very apprehensive. I was worried that I might be mistaken as an escapee, and summarily executed. Luckily, I saw a glimmer of light in the distance, and headed eagerly in that direction. Finally, I reached the source of light. It was an electrician with a lantern who was inspecting the light system on the field. I followed him back to my shelter. All the members of my squad had returned safely. I was the last one.

The storm continued until the next morning, followed by several days of drizzle. The water level of the Huai River and Poyang Lake rose quickly, submerging all of our unfinished excavation. Our bloody toil had washed away. Continuation of the project was impossible. We felt somewhat relieved since we would get a short rest. I washed my clothes and hung them outside to dry, where they were stolen. In order to have another change of clothes, I sewed a pair of pants and shirt out of a blanket. Since I did not know how to sew, my new "clothes" were ill-fitting and funny-looking. My odd outfit did not elicit any stares or sneers. Nobody cared.

During this period between "jobs," our only activity was reeducation, one session in the morning, another in the afternoon. The topics were domestic and international affairs, Party and government policies, and a critical review of our personal lives. Because there was no physical work, our exhaustion gradually retreated. But a new pest emerged – a multitude of flies and mosquitoes. The flies worked the day shift, while the mosquitoes did their work at night. We were amused that the flies and mosquitoes had adopted our two-shift system. When you picked up a bun, you first had to shake off the flies. The proliferation of flies and mosquitoes was due to the overflowing latrines caused by the deluge of rain. Since the latrines could no longer be used, we ten thousand human beings defecated anywhere and everywhere—in the bushes, around the walls, by the roadside, and even around the shelters. The mosquitoes were the devils of the night, their buzz preventing sleep and their bites spreading malaria. Since we had no mosquito nets, we had to cover ourselves from head to toe with blankets or clothes. The only way to relieve the itching was to die of malaria!

THE MOVE TO NORTHERN JIANGSU PROVINCE

Two weeks later they announced that we would be departing for our new project in a few days. They did not tell us where we were going, but said we would be doing farm work. We would plant grains and vegetables, learning how to live an agricultural life of propriety and contentment. We were warned that rules and regulations must be strictly followed en route. Any violation or attempt to flee would be dealt with harshly. We looked forward to our life on the farm – it had to be an improvement over the canal project.

After a few more quiet days, we were told to pack up. The packing of my few belongings took less than thirty minutes. I sat in the shade, waiting for the order to leave. After it was given, we walked in columns of four.

Although it had not rained for over a week, the ground was still muddy, making it tiring to walk. After passing a small village, we reached a riverbank where a string of boats was waiting. The sun was setting, but there was still enough light for us to see the armed guards with bayonets along both sides of the river. We were crowded onto the small boats, so tightly that we had to stand throughout the journey. We landed the next morning, and went ashore lined up in rows to get our food. Thirsty and without water, we could barely swallow the dry buns.

After the meal, we set out on the road. After standing in the boats all night, we were exhausted, and the backpacks felt heavier than ever. After an hour, many of the weaker ones fell behind. The armed guards ran back and forth, prodding the laggards along. Sometimes, they used a whip to speed them up, but these prisoners were too debilitated to keep up. The line grew longer and longer and fell into disorder. My physical capacity was average, and with my light backpack (thanks to the theft of my clothing) I managed with effort to stay in the middle of the pack. All of a sudden, I heard gunfire at the back of the line.

Then I heard, "Hurry. If you walk too slowly, you will be shot to death."

I walked as fast as I could and finally, dawn broke – I had lived to see another day. It soon turned blazingly bright. The head of the line suddenly stopped. Those who were in the back gradually caught up. The brigadiers announced that we had reached our destination—the Reform Farm of Binhai County in northern Jiangsu Province. Another chapter.

CHAPTER 5

FARM WORK IN NORTHERN JIANGSU

FROM WASTELAND TO COTTON FIELDS

In Binhai County, we initially stayed at a high school. The classrooms were empty because of summer vacation. We slept on the desks and used the stools as tables for our meals. This was the best housing since my arrest. At the time of our arrival, the shelters on the farm were still under construction, which is why we had a few days at the high school.

Our final destination was the Xinnan Company, about ten kilometers east of the county. The "New South Company" was a deserted cotton plantation. Zhang Jian, a zhuangyuan (the highest graduate of the Chinese Imperial Examination) in the late Qing Dynasty, went from a scholar to entrepreneur, acquiring this land for growing cotton at the beginning of the Chinese Republic. The cotton supplied his two textile factories in his hometown of Nantong. Tidal waves over the years eventually rendered the land sterile. The government had sent us to reclaim this large plantation.

While we were settling in, we talked about the gunfire that we heard the night before. We speculated on what had happened. Perhaps the guards had shot those who had fallen too far behind, or perhaps they had shot those who were attempting to flee. Under these circumstances, a criminal carried less weight than an animal.

During the week at Binhai High School, I came down with malaria. There was no medical care. The cadres showed very little concern. Since we had not yet been assigned any work, I was able to rest and regain some of my strength. A few days later, we walked the ten kilometers to the shelter. Two good-hearted fellow prisoners carried some of my things. Because of the hot weather, we were given two rest stops. The journey would not have been too hard if I hadn't been sick, but due to my malaria, I collapsed upon reaching our destination.

The place assigned to us was not the Xinnan Company proper but an adjacent piece of land, about 200 square meters. Surrounding it were rivers

40 meters wide; our land was an island. A wooden bridge connected the island to the highway. Armed guards manned security posts along the river and the bridge. Our shelters were built with coarse wood and rushes, in the shape of the letter "A." We slept on wooden boards. The space allocated for each person was a disappointing 30 centimeter wide, no better than what we had at Huai River. The water was not potable because of the repeated tidal waves. The water, whether from the river or wells, was salty. The more you drank, the thirstier you became; the thirstier you became, the more you wanted to drink. Clothing washed in brine was greasy, smelly, and itchy. As the days went by, our health deteriorated. I got thinner and weaker, eventually too tired to walk.

In the early stages, there was no farm work. We were assigned to cut down the thick, dense rushes. The reason for cutting down the rushes was twofold: the rushes were used to build more shelters, and the cleared land –after being drained of saltwater—could be used to grow cotton.

The clearing of the rushes started near the shelter and then moved to the outer regions. We formed an assembly line of sorts. Each squad undertook a section. Some did the cutting; others bundled the rushes up into little pyramids. The depth of the ponds varied from ankle-deep to knee-deep. To cut the rushes we had to stand in the water, where we worked more than ten hours a day. Lunch was brought to us, which we had to eat standing up. During the summer, the workday started early and drew to a close until dark. The authorities would never let us stop as long as there was still some daylight.

After three months of cutting, we had cleared a vast area of land. It was now early December and the weather was cold. To reach the cutting area, we had to pass through a big swamp where the water was waist-deep. We shivered as we plunged into the water in the morning and evening. Many in my squad fell sick. I seemed to be endowed with more tolerance for cold, and my health held up.

One day, the weather took a sudden turn for the worse. The north wind raged. Snowflakes fell. A thin layer of ice formed on the swamp, barring us from working. In the evening, the office notified me to pick up a parcel. This message gave me a moment of warmth—someone somewhere still cared about me. I went to the office to pick up my package. When I was walking back, I slipped in the snow, scattering the contents of the package. I was too weak to stand up. A fellow prisoner helped me up, gathered the contents of my package, and accompanied me back to the shelter.

The package was from my father. It contained a used lined coverlet and a few pieces of old clothing. Undoubtedly, it was all they could spare. The package also included a letter from my father giving me the sad news that my mother had died from heart disease. On her deathbed, she had picked out a few items for him to send me. Her dying wish was for me to work diligently in order to earn some leniency and return home sooner. My father asked me not to mourn too much because mourning would be harmful to my health and interfere with my ability to work hard so that I might return home sooner. I cried like a baby for my mother.

The next morning, when I woke up, I found my limbs numb and paralyzed. I could not stand up or move my arms. My fingers were so stiff that they could not hold a pair of chopsticks. According to the doctor, it was caused by frequent and long immersion in water. The symptoms were aggravated by the sudden change in the weather. In the beginning of this illness, I had to be assisted in everything—even eating and excretion. This devastating loss of autonomy and dignity depressed me. Luckily, a few days later, the weather turned warmer and I started to recover. My arms began to move, my hands could grasp, and I could walk by leaning against a wall.

During this time, the supervisor notified us to stop cutting the rushes. Our new task was to dig drainage trenches to remove the saltwater from the land—to make the land arable. The whole group moved to Chenjiagang, on the coast. Because of my partial paralysis, I was allowed to remain for a lighter assignment of mixing decaying organic matter into fertilizer.

Before the trenches could be dug, the weather took a sudden turn for the worse. A violent northwest wind caused a sudden drop in temperature. Just about the time that everybody had gone to bed, an urgent call came from the office. A battalion of prisoners from Fujian province, on an assignment to move provisions from a commune warehouse, was stuck in the snowstorm. All the laborers from our farm must try to rescue them. In less than fifteen minutes, all the able-bodied prisoners were on their way. As one of the invalids, I did not go on this mission, but I remained awake worrying about the fate of the Fujian battalion.

Finally, at dawn, the rescue mission straggled back to camp. I asked the man lying next to me how many people he rescued and who they were. He answered, "I am not sure. Many had already frozen to death by the time

Chapter 5 *Farm Work in Northern Jiangsu*

the rescue party arrived."

He also said, "Fujian is in the tropical zone. People there usually do not have clothing for cold weather. They could not sustain this sudden cold and took refuge in shelters. They did not realize that once idle, they could not even stand up. After a while, they froze to death." When I asked for more details, he did not respond. I then, of course, stopped being inquisitive. Later, I was informed that the commander had ordered them not to talk about the freezing deaths.

Despite this tragic event, the authorities acted as if nothing had happened. The very next day, the group assigned to do the trench and drainage work left for their worksite. Less than ten of us – the sick and elderly –stayed behind to do the composting. Our group included a well-known jurist, Mr. Sheng, who had been a legislator under the Nationalist government and the dean of the law school of X University; Mr. Tang, the Chancellor of Y University of Zhejiang Province; and Dr. Lou, a Ph.D. electrical engineer. There was also a deputy director of the Bureau of Information of the Nationalist government, whose name I forget, and Mr. Xing, a history instructor at Beijing University.

Our erudite composting squad made fertilizer by collecting withered grass, molded leaves, dead animals, feces, manure, and other decayed organic matter; watering this stew; and sealing it with mud. I was assigned to pick up manure, not a job for the faint of heart—but at least it gave me freedom of movement. Carrying a basket on my back, I went anywhere I wanted. Time passed easily with this type of work. This faeces and manure gathering was in fact the most pleasant labor I performed throughout all the years of reform through labor.

As summer approached, the mosquitoes flourished. Their humming and biting disrupted our sleep. We tried to smoke them away by burning leaves, but the smoke bothered us more than the mosquitoes. A prisoner in another brigade committed an undisclosed misdemeanor for which the punishment was lying naked and left to the ravages of the mosquitoes. By morning, he had become unconscious. Shortly thereafter, he died.

The trench work was completed during the summer. Our composting squad was disbanded. Mr. Sun, a former member of the squad, remained in the same brigade with me. All the other members went back to their own squads and were later transferred away, leaving my life forever. Mr. Sun, a college graduate, and I became friends. Friendship was perilous, as a close association between prisoners could be looked upon as a conspiracy. One day I saw that Mr. Sun was not at work. I thought he must be ill. But on my return to the shelter, I learned that an armed dispatch from the south had taken him away handcuffed behind his back. I never found out what unkind fate greeted him. I missed my friend.

WORDS THAT LED TO DISASTER

One day, headquarters assembled us and announced that the North Jiangsu Farm would begin farming operations after the trench and drainage work was done. Besides planting cotton, we would plant grains and vegetables. We were told to conclude our work and prepare for departure, which would take place in a few days.

Three days later, we left for our new place. Our battalion belonged to the first detachment that was to go to Xinan proper. Its new name was North Jiangsu Farm I. The detachment consisted of five battalions, about five thousand men. The second detachment was to go to the Xintong Company, which was called North Jiangsu Farm II. New Nan proper was only ten kilometers from our present station, but there were no connecting roads. In addition, channels and trenches crisscrossed the field, making our trek quite arduous.

North Jiangsu Farm No. 1 was reclaimed from rush ponds, a barren piece of land. A group of reform laborers had gone ahead and made some improvements: shelters had been built, vegetable fields planted, pigpens and a pantry established. Our job was to plow the fields. There were twelve people to a plow. Each group was expected to plow two *mu* (about 1/6th of an acre) each day. Although the rush had been cleared, the roots were intertwined under the ground, making the plowing extremely difficult. We could not even complete one *mu* per day. The supervisors reduced our work quota to one *mu* per day, but if half a *mu* was not completed by noon, there would be no lunch. The other half had to be completed before we were released for the day. Oftentimes, we had to work until seven o'clock, returning to the shelter in darkness.

Because most of the battalions could not meet their quota of one *mu*, the managers of the farm called a general meeting to push for more productivity. They asked us to acknowledge our guilt and demonstrate our law-abiding spirit by working harder. They made it clear that the government would reward or punish every person according to his performance.

The speaker, chairman of the board of Farm No. 1, concluded by saying, "The Communist Party takes everything seriously. Once it decides to do something, nothing is impossible. In order to achieve a goal, the Party does not care how many sacrifices it has to make."

When we got back to the shelter, I grumbled, "The Party is prepared to make any sacrifice as long as it is us, the prisoners, making the sacrifices." Right after I spoke, I regretted my poorly chosen words. I was afraid of being reported.

As expected, the next evening the officer of the battalion summoned me.

"Do you know why we called you in?" he asked coldly.

"No."

"What did you say last night?" he pressed.

Even though I knew what he was referring to, I feigned ignorance.

"I did not say anything." I said, "I can't think of anything."

"You did not say anything? It was only yesterday. How can you forget what you said? Someone made an accusation against you. I'll read it to you. 'Last night after supper, Mr. X, in front of all of us, said, "The Communist Party, for the sake of achieving an end, does not care how much sacrifice other people have to bear.' Did you say that?"

I was frightened. "That was not the way I said it. It has been twisted."

He replied, "Your remarks reflected your resentment against the Party. Doesn't it totally reflect your reactionary way of thinking?"

My resentment was a fact. I could not deny it. To further dissemble would only make things worse. I lowered my head in shame and kept silent. He took my dropped head and silence as a sign of repentance. He continued,

"You can go back. Within a couple of days, write a letter of self-criticism and submit it to me. We will see whether you have awakened from your error and resolved to change. Then we will decide how to handle the case."

After I returned to the shelter, my fellow prisoners asked me why I was called in. I told them I had been given some paperwork to do. Of course, the one who turned me in knew exactly why I was called in.

The next day, I wrote a letter of self-criticism in a formulaic manner and brought it to the office. The same officer was there alone.

He read the letter and asked, "Is this all you have learned?"

"Yes," I said.

"You have taken it too lightly," he said. "If I forward this letter to a higher level, things will go badly for you. You are well-educated, which makes your case even more serious. This time I will take your remark as a slip of the tongue and not treat it as an intentional attack. Do not make the same mistake again. If you do, it will be taken as a deliberate act. Both offenses will be taken together and you will be severely punished."

I nodded and walked out of the office. I had not expected the case to go so smoothly. I tried to analyze this auspicious turn of events. First, the officer was an enlightened, reasonable person. Second, he already had a good impression of me because I had done some paperwork for him several times with which he was satisfied. Third, both times when I was in his office he was alone. He had complete freedom to make the disposition as he saw fit.

Oftentimes, one wrong word could be considered an attack on the Party, resulting in punishment by self-criticism in one's own group and even at an assembly where one was publicly repudiated. Punishments could include confinement, additional demerits, and extension of one's prison term. This time none of this occurred, but I did not know whether the report, my self-criticism, and the disposition would be kept on file. If a file had been created, this record could prevent my life from ever returning to normal.

From then on, I became more guarded in my speech, keeping my opinions to myself. I avoided political discussions. I avoided offending anyone. While I was not by nature timorous, I was forced to change for my very survival.

After the farm-wide assembly, battalion meetings followed, then meetings of the brigades and discussions within the squads. Everyone was compelled to speak out, to show his willingness to participate in farm labor, to write letters of determination, letters of assurance, and letters of challenge and acceptance. These activities were repetitious and redundant. Their purpose was to extract more work out of the prisoners. But the prisoners were worn out; there was nothing left for the supervisors to exploit.

ESCAPE PLANS

The weather got warmer. On May 1st, International Labor Day for the Communist world, the supervisors called a "Reward and Punishment" meeting. We all looked forward to having our sentences reduced at this meeting. Our hopes were dashed when only twelve prisoners out of 10,000 had their sentence reduced, and their terms were only reduced by six to twelve months. On the other hand, long additional sentences were inflicted on many prisoners. We realized that malevolence was all we could expect from our masters.

No wonder the number of escape attempts escalated sharply. The supervisors did not disclose escape attempts unless the person was caught. There were two circles of guards around the farm. The number of posts was inadequate, so it was not too difficult for prisoners to slip across the guarded lines. The problem was that even if you escaped, you would not be able to establish a foothold in any community.

The Communists had set up neighborhood surveillance groups in every urban and rural area. Without proper status, you would surely be caught under the glare of public scrutiny. In addition, escapees with no money or ration coupons would not be able to survive. The only escapees with a reasonable chance of surviving were those who were talented thieves. They could hide out from one community to another, stealing what they needed. Those who were caught trying to escape were executed.

In one case, the escapee slipped through the guarded line. When he was discovered, the guards riddled his body with machine gun fire. The other case was even more dramatic. Three prisoners, after stealing two sets of cadre uniforms and forging a document with the official seal, acted as two cadres who were escorting a prisoner to the county office. Because the document did not fully conform to official ones, this crafty plot was detected at the gate. The three prisoners were sentenced to death. The execution took place in an open field. We were all ordered to witness the execution. One of the three was a college student, very imposing in stature and appearance. He was in the battalion which had access to the uniforms and official seal. Before the execution, the prisoners were handcuffed behind their backs, waiting for their judgments to be read. They held up their heads proudly. The first shots failed to kill them; follow-up shots were necessary.

Since the "Reward and Punishment" meeting, our morale had reached a nadir. We now realized that reduction of our sentences was a fantasy, whereas an increase was a real possibility. At the prison, judgments rendered for minor offenses were often ten, fifteen, or twenty years. I knew I would never be released early and that I would be over fifty years old before I was released. Probably everyone in my family would be dead by then. Moreover, life in labor camp was so unbearable that I did not see how I could survive that long. So, I also thought of escape; what did I have to lose? The idea preoccupied me. I thought carefully and in minute detail on this matter—what time to escape, how to escape, and how to prepare for my escape attempt.

The first decision I made was to escape alone. Any accomplice might betray me for his own benefit. Even if I was successful in escaping the farm camp, I would still be in the larger prison: China. Hong Kong or Macau was my best hope. But to get there, I would have to travel a long inland route. With no money or documents, anything could happen to me. So in the end, I decided I had to leave China by sea.

The farm was on the coast of Jiangsu, only ten kilometers from the harbor of Chenjiagang, where I had once carried a load of radishes from Shandong.[1] Facing an immense sea, Chenjiagang was sparsely populated. Along the shore was a big, unpopulated salt field, a good place from which to leave the country. My plan was to steal some leftover rice from the pantry and hide it in my pillowcase for provisions. Then I would slip out of the farm in the dark with my bed sheet and filled pillowcase, and find a wooden board for a flotation device. I would tie the sheet to a bamboo stick for my sail. To the east of North Jiangsu was the southern tip of the Korean peninsula. On its southeastern end were the Kyushu and Ryukyu Islands of Japan, only a few hundred kilometers away. With a favorable wind, it would take about twelve days to reach one of those islands. In the summer, the water would not be too cold. I would live on my stolen rice.

I was elated with this novel plan. But just when I was scouting my surroundings and waiting for an opportune moment, I saw that I was

---

[1] Chenjiagang (simplified Chinese: 陈家港镇; traditional Chinese: 陳家港鎮; pinyin: Chénjiāgǎng zhèn) literally means "Chen family port" and is a town in Jiangsu Province of China.

basing the escape on the assumption of favorable winds. If the wind was against me, the result would be entirely different. In China, the wind usually blew from the southeast during summer and northwest in the winter. But the southeast wind of summer would pin me to the coast. The northwest wind that I needed for my escape only occurred in the winter, at a time when the cold sea would freeze me to death. With this closer analysis, I realized that my elegant escape plan was doomed. I would remain a prisoner.

INJURY

At about this time, I suffered a serious injury. One day, the office handed down a special assignment to cut out the grass roots in order to cultivate vegetables. This was a very difficult and taxing job because the roots were strongly intertwined in the soil like a piece of carpet.

I had to use a specially forged steel shovel that was 40 cm long and 10 cm wide, with pointed angles on both sides, and a sharp tip. In the shape of a crescent, the instrument seemed like an ancient weapon. To cut through the roots, I had to plunge the shovel into the ground with great force. But I slipped and fell, resulting in the pointed angle of the shovel cutting the back of my left foot. I cried out in pain and fell down.

Fellow workers immediately came to my rescue. They carried me to the clinic. The doctor immediately applied a tourniquet, stemming the gushing blood. He cleaned, disinfected, and bandaged the wound, hoping to prevent an infection. He wrapped it with a thick bandage.

I asked, "Why is it wrapped so heavily?"

"It is to prevent any bacteria from entering the wound. It will be very dangerous if it gets infected." I was then carried to my shelter.

Next morning, the doctor came to tell me that I had been granted one week's leave. He asked me to go to the clinic in three days for a dressing change. The supervisors were usually very tightfisted about granting leaves. This time, the doctor must have played a very important role in allowing me a long rest. On the third day, with assistance, I went to the clinic for a dressing change. I attempted to remove the bandages myself but was immediately stopped by the doctor. He told me that if I did that, the closure of the wound might break open, and I might lose my foot.

He dripped warm water onto the bandage, gradually loosening the adherent gauze. He untied the bandage one layer after another. The appearance of my foot startled me. The front part of my foot was dark purple. The doctor told me this was due to clotted blood from the broken veins. If the veins healed and the circulation came back, the color of my foot would return to normal. If not, then part or all of my foot would have to be amputated.

I worried about how I could carry on if I became crippled. Would I be given lighter work or would I simply be shot since I was no longer useful?

The week passed. I was far from being able to return to the fields. Fortunately, two additional people were needed to slice the radishes. At the suggestion of the doctor, I was assigned to be a radish chopper. After about a month, my wound completely healed and I could walk normally. I was not crippled.

The good outcome of my foot injury was due to many fortuitous circumstances. First, the accident occurred close to the clinic and I was carried there immediately after the injury. Second, when I arrived at the clinic, both the doctor and the nurse was present and not occupied with other patients, enabling them to quickly attend to me. Third, my fellow prisoners were very sympathetic. During my recuperation, they assisted me in every possible way. Fourth, I had a good rapport with the doctor. We had played chess together on his days off. He was very attentive and arranged to have the long recuperation that I needed. The doctor was my friend during my time of need; I shall always remember him with profound gratitude. His family name was Xun, a rare surname in Chinese genealogy.

Although I was not disabled from the injury, overexertion would cause severe pain in my left foot. The growth of an osteophyte on my left big toe was another aftermath of this accident. Whenever I see this bony spur, I am reminded of my accident and the ordeals of prison life.

EXPOSE THE REBELS

It was summer. Except for plowing, there was nothing new. The routine on the farm was dull and suffocating.

Suddenly, the commander announced a new work schedule. He emphasized that the great government policy of reform through labor was a balance between productive labor and ideological reeducation. At the end of the meeting, we were asked to stand up and shout "Long Live the Great People's Republic of China! Long Live the Great Chinese Communist Party! Long Live Our Great Leader Chairman Mao."

Back at the brigade, a meeting was immediately held to announce the new schedule. The brigadier general made a lengthy speech in which he said that the necessity of getting the farm up and running had required an emphasis on labor rather than learning. Now that the land had been reclaimed and the farm was operational, there would be time for reeducation after the evening meal. Roll call would be made at the assembly and the day's work would be reviewed. Those who had performed well would be acclaimed; those who had performed poorly would be criticized and might receive demerits or additional penalties. They would be expected to undergo strict self-examination of their unsatisfactory performance. The learning sessions would run from 7 to 9. The topics would include politics, current affairs, international and domestic situations, the writings of Chairman Mao, the reform through labor policy, a comparison of socialism and capitalism, and the inevitability of the east wind prevailing over the west wind. We would study by taking classes, listening to reports, reading documents and newspapers, group discussions, taking notes, mutual assistance, self-criticism, being criticized by others, and so on. Furthermore, we were urged to report bad people.

While the new schedule resulted in less physical labor, mental torture was greatly increased. At the meetings, prisoners were encouraged to criticize one another. I was appointed group leader, which meant that I had to take notes on everything that was said. The brigadier general and the cadres kept me under surveillance. In the meantime, the battalion decided that we must learn the revolutionary songs, asking musical prisoners to teach the others. One of the songs was an ode to Mao and the

Chinese Communist Party. It said that we the reform laborers must be grateful to Chairman Mao and the Communist Party, who gave us the opportunity to be reborn. We were ordered to sing that song before every meal. Just like the Christians who pray, Mao was trying put himself in the same place as God.

All the laborers—except for the few assigned to construction, sanitation, health clinic, animal husbandry, and the kitchen—were plowing and cultivating. By the following spring, over thirty thousand mu had been cultivated. Tractors were sent in for the plowing. Our work turned to digging trenches and flattening the plowed ground for planting the seeds. This went on for about two months until the beginning of summer.

One day after breakfast, when we were ready to go to work, an order was issued that work was cancelled and that we would have a farm-wide assembly instead. Once the meeting started, no one would be allowed to leave. The service laborers held all kinds of posters in their hands, containing slogans such as: "Crack the Counterrevolutionary Insurrection Gang," "Strike the Anti-reform Elements," "Resolutely Extinguish the Enemies of the People," "Fiercely Strike the Insurrection Elements," "No Rest until Total Victory," and "Prosecute and Disclose, Do Not Let a Single Evil One Slip Out of the Net." In the meantime, a number of soldiers from the Liberation Army gathered. Prisoners talked stealthily to one other. We were ordered to line up in double columns on the vacant field. But they still had not told us what the meeting was for.

When we arrived, many of the battalions were already sitting on the ground. There was a temporary wooden platform draped with banners at the end of the field. The words were similar to those we had seen already. Many cadres were sitting on the platform, few of whom I recognized. The same slogans were shouted by the crowd. Everyone was required to shout them out with one hand raised. The undulation of hands looked like a storm in the ocean. Armed soldiers from the Liberation Army were all around. It was in this bellicose atmosphere that the meeting was called to order.

An officer announced that a large counterrevolutionary gang of insurrectionists had been detected. They plan to plunder weapons and ammunition from the security troops, kill cadres, and burn warehouses. They also plan to slip into various communities, seeking hidden opposition forces for widening the movement. The conspiracy started at the time of the Spring Festival. The government immediately learned of this secret plan but decided to just watch the gang first, waiting until all the accomplices could be rounded up in a single stroke. The government believed the time is now. This meeting had been called to arrest the principles of this conspiratorial organization right here and now.

Then roll call was made. Afterward, those accused were called and dragged to the platform, handcuffed behind their backs. Over ten were accused. Although several thousand people were at the meeting, the place was dead silent. The actions of the authorities were no different than taking turtles from a jar.

Those who were called were powerless to resist arrest. Had they even committed these crimes? After the ten or so were arrested, the officers whispered to each other. It looked like that they were discussing something of importance. There was a strained stillness.

After a while, the previous officer spoke again, "Those who were just arrested were the principles of the insurrection gang. They are the deadly enemies of the people, the black sheep of the reform through labor camps. They did not make a judicious assessment of their own power and attempted the impossible task of switching their loyalties. Their final fate is something we will soon witness. Notwithstanding the fact that the government has information from those who were persuaded or seduced into that attempt, it does not want to take any action against them at this moment. The government wants to know whether they are resolved to deplore their own sins, disclose accomplices, and make a voluntary openhearted confession. Those involved should never think that their case is not serious enough to warrant arrest. The Party and the government, with the benevolent policy of healing the sick and salvaging the drowning, are willing to extend extreme leniency. Make a clear assessment of the situation, trust the government, and salvage others while reclaiming yourselves." Those arrested were then tied together and led away.

Afterward, the Counselor for Disciplinary Affairs then instructed us on how each battalion should conduct its learning programs. He urged prisoners to scrutinize each other and to report suspicious characters. The meeting lasted until midday. All the brigades followed the soldiers from the Liberation Army and the armed guards off the field.

The brigade held a meeting that night. The counselor in charge arranged for all the squads to conduct learning sessions according to the spirit that had been expounded at the assembly. Everyone was required to speak out and lay bare his attitude. As the discussion progressed, confession, prosecution, and disclosure should take place. The counselor stressed that there should be no fear of retaliation or revenge when making accusations and disclosures; the government would keep the identity of the accuser confidential. Those who did a good job would be duly rewarded. Everyone was urged to boldly confront suspects. There should be no fear of wrongfully implicating innocent parties; the government would carefully verify each case. While no single wrongdoer would go unpunished, neither would any false prosecution be made.

Finally, he warned, "Those who were arrested are under strict surveillance. In order to benefit from a more gracious disposition, they will confess about their associates. Those involved will be treated leniently if they take the initiative and bravely confess. If crimes are disclosed by others instead of by self-denunciation, then the disposition will be much more severe. This opportunity for leniency will soon pass. Do not miss it."

The break-up of the insurrectionists and the arrest of the principles filled us with terror. I was particularly apprehensive because I knew one of the men who had been arrested. His name was Fei; he was from my hometown. He was a bright-eyed intellectual, short in stature but handsome. I first met him when I was returning from work. I was talking to a Mr. Sun in my native dialect. Someone approached me and asked, "Are you from Suzhou?"

I said, "Yes."

He said, "I heard you speaking in the Suzhou dialect, so I assumed you are from Suzhou. So am I. We are fellow townsmen."

After that conversation, he told me his name and I gave him mine. I remembered that the Fei family was one of the eminent clans in our town and that they were old family friends.

"Does Mr. So-and-So belong to your family?" I asked.

"Yes, he is one of my distant uncles."

After this short encounter, I met him once more after work. During that second meeting, we conversed about our reeducation and work experience, our cases, and some past events in Suzhou. Ever since I had been warned about wrongful speech and submitted a letter of self-criticism, I had been taking great care in my conversations. Therefore, with Mr. Fei I tried not to expose too much of myself and my thoughts, especially my views on political matters and current affairs. Because we did not belong to the same battalion, and our shelters and work areas were far apart, we did not meet again.

Now that he had been arrested as one of the ringleaders of the insurrection gang, I was worried that under coercion, he might falsely implicate me so that he might win favorable disposition for his case. I fluctuated between taking the initiative to report our encounters to not calling attention to them. To report it first might have the advantage of preempting a possible prosecution. But on second thought, even though we knew each other, I knew nothing about his organization or his activities. A voluntary report might arouse suspicion. I decided to sit tight.

A week later another meeting of the whole farm was called. This time, I knew that the meeting could have grave consequences for me. If Mr. Fei had implicated me as one of the conspirators, I would be handcuffed and plucked out of the flock. Under the policy of "lenient to those who confess open-heartedly, merciless to those who resist confession; prosecution and disclosure will be rewarded based on meritorious services," there had been numerous cases of intentional exaggeration of other's roles in crimes and accusing innocent parties in order to gain lenient disposition.

The meeting was called to order. After a period of slogan chanting, an officer made a speech, "After the last meeting, all battalions expanded their discussions for the purpose of breaking up the conspiratorial gang of insurrection. Confessions and prosecutions are underway. Some of the culprits and their associates elevated their thinking, trusted the government, and relieved their burden of guilt by initiating a truthful confession. That was a good sign. The government would definitely extend the most considerate treatment or even exemption to anyone confessing his guilt. But there are still participants who have not voluntarily confessed, and instead, are hoping in vain to fool the government. Fortunately, the government has documented their misdeeds as clearly as their noses. Now we will call out their names for arrest."

He then shouted, "So-and-so from X squad of Y brigade, stand up!"

As soon as the order was given, armed guards dragged the prisoner to the platform and handcuffed him. I was terrified that my name would be called. After nine arrests, the calls stopped. I had not been called.

The same officer further expounded, "The government determines penalties on the basis of two factors: one, the gravity of the criminal activity; and two, the culprit's readiness to confess during the course of the investigation. A criminal with grave misconduct who confesses openheartedly with repentance, or who discloses guilty parties, will receive consideration for a more lenient disposition. On the other hand, a perpetrator of misdemeanors who stubbornly refuses to admit his crime may incur severe punishment. 'Lenient to those who confess openheartedly and merciless to those who resist' is the brilliant and immutable policy of the government. The few people who were just taken are examples you should not follow. We want you to draw a lesson from the two meetings that have been held, and make an early confession of your involvement with the case. You only have a limited time to act. Do not let the opportunity slip away." The meeting ended at dusk.

Since my arrest, I had heard these urgings ten or fifteen times. After this meeting, my tension eased somewhat. I was consoled and filled with gratitude that Mr. Fei had not dragged me into the noxious pool. I admired his generosity and courage in absorbing the ordeal without involving innocent people. Of course, I could not be sure that he would continue to resist the pressure of implicating others. I could still be vulnerable.

As a participant or even the initiator of this rebellious group, he had shown that he was not a coward. On the other hand, I was not completely free of apprehension, even though I was lucky enough to pass the ominous test twice. I could not be sure that I would not be involved in a later round. As the policy announcer had said, "The government was determined to smash the entire ring. There would be no rest until total victory."

One day, I did not go to work because of illness. I was lying at one end of the shelter. At the other end of the shelter, thirty meters away, lay another sick worker. A uniformed middle-aged man who appeared to be a cadre came in with a briefcase. He first talked to the other man. Because of the distance, I could not hear them. Then he came to me and asked why I had not gone to work. I told him that I was on sick leave. I assumed that he was one of the cadres who was inspecting the service conditions. I tried to show him my certificate of leave. He waved his hand to show that he did not want to see it. Then he asked me my name, age, domicile, education, experience, and the details of my case.

After I had answered all of his questions, he told me, "In the face of misfortune, you are lucky that you can do farm work after being sentenced to a twelve-year term. According to the original policy, prisoners with a term of more than ten years were to be executed. Later, based on the benevolent spirit of healing the sick and salvaging the drowning, the government softened the policy into a reform-through-labor program. You should be grateful to the government, work hard, learn diligently, reform with a keen sense of error, and turn to a new chapter of your life." His tone was tender and kind.

He then left, but I felt some misgivings about his visit. How could a cadre speak so softly to a prisoner and reveal to me the secret policy of the state? I assumed that his words were out of sympathy, to give me some consolation and encouragement. But his insinuation that the government changed its policy based on humanitarian considerations seemed a bit far-fetched. Since the Communists had come to power, a series of oppressive measures, such as the planned implications, the Great Search and Arrest, the large scale imprisonments, and the mass executions, had taken place one after the other. There did not seem to be a trace of humanitarian consideration.

If what he said about the policy change was true, I could only gather that the Communists had changed policy based on economic rather than humanitarian considerations. Because many pressing and difficult projects, such as embankment and irrigation, highway and railroad construction, mine exploration, and land reclamation were underway, prisoners as laborers were more useful than executed prisoners.

Later, I heard that the prison authority in Shanghai had sent a team to inspect the conditions in the labor camps. I assumed that the person who talked to me in the shelter was one of those officers. No doubt he knew what had been brewing in the Shanghai prison. I had planned to tell this secret to those friendly to me. But I chose not to do so because I knew this was a very serious matter. If the word was passed onto the authorities, it might incite another mischief. The government definitely would make a thorough investigation on the source of the information. Not only would I get into trouble, but it would also implicate the good-hearted officer.

Fall arrived. The case of conspiratorial insurrection subsided but was not settled. Disposition had yet to be given to the two batches of the accused. I was still worried that Mr. Fei might implicate me. One day, at a battalion meeting, the officer announced a list of prisoners who were going to be sent west to build railroads. My name was on it. This was great news because the transfer proved that I had not been implicated in the insurrection case. As to what railroad building would be like, I could care less. Here I had witnessed the shooting of escapees, the arrest of insurrectionists, ceaseless "education" meetings, frequent exhortation for prosecution and disclosure, and coerced confessions. I couldn't wait to say goodbye to this place.

CHAPTER 6

RAILROAD WORK IN THE WEST

BAWANG RIVER BRIDGE

The following morning the prisoners chosen for railroad work were asked to pack up and be ready to depart. I was feeling quite positive about the transfer. Even if the new job were tedious, perhaps the psychological infliction would be less. Shortly after noon, we were summoned. We lined up in columns and walked to the parade ground.

We then marched for three hours on a smooth road, reaching our destination for the day. Hundreds of prisoners conscripted from different battalions were already there. The next morning, an assembly was called. Each of us was given a quilted cover and two sets of clothes, one lined and one unlined. Though not of good quality, at least they were new. We were thrilled and delighted. For the past three and a half years, we had not received any government issue. Most of our clothes were torn and ragged. When I was first arrested, I had a long quilted gown with silk batting. After it was torn, I shortened it into a vest. My coverlet was also threadbare. It no longer fully covered my body. The new sets of clothes were one of the high points of my thirty years in captivity.

According to my reasoning, to go westward from north Jiangsu, a straighter and shorter route was by way of Haizhou, now the city of Lianyungang. The route we took was to go to Huaiyin by boat, then down through the Grand Canal and across the Yangtze to reach Zhenjiang. We stayed at the prison of Zhenjiang for about ten days.

The Zhenjiang Prison contained only female prisoners, mostly young. After not seeing women for years, this sudden exposure naturally induced some feelings of lust. If it were not for the strict rules against contact between the male and female prisoners, some prison "romances" would surely have ensued.

We stayed in the newly built prison factory, a reinforced concrete building, big and bright. Water and electricity had been installed; machinery was yet to be installed. Bedding was placed on hay, which was rather comfortable. The cadres did not give us any work or learning

Chapter 6 *Railroad Work in the West*

assignments. We had two rather decent meals a day and plenty of leisure time. Some slept, some played chess, some read, and others strolled around the garden. The Zhenjiang prison had a garden with a pond, artificial hills, and a pavilion. Not as prison-like, it had been built to house female prisoners. They were not treated as harshly as male prisoners.

After ten days of this pleasure, the notice for departure came. Everyone packed hurriedly and waited to set out. We walked to a substation and boarded a freight car. We were comfortable, as the car was not overcrowded. We passed Nanjing, Xuzhou, Jinan, Tianjin, and Beijing - finally reaching the destination Jining. Why we had to go this roundabout way was something I could not explain. The entire trip from Binhai to Jining took more than thirty days. Aside from the ten-day pause at Zhenjiang, the boat ride from Binhai to Zhenjiang was unusually long. The underpowered steamship with ten trailing boats was very slow. But we didn't care; reaching the destination earlier would only have meant that hard labor would soon begin.

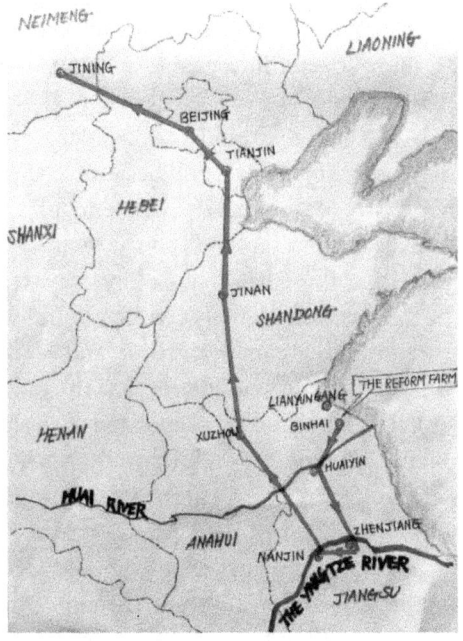

Jining of the Inner Mongolia Autonomous Region, on the Beijing-Baotou Railroad, is the southernmost point of the Jining-Erlianhaote Railroad. Erlianhaote, at its northern end, is on the China-Mongolia border. Farther north is the People's Republic of Mongolia. The entire road is on the crevice of the bordering mountain. Because the cold Siberian winds pass through Outer Mongolia into China, it is severely cold in the winter. This time, we were placed around the abutment under the railroad bridge that lies over the Bawang River. The A-shaped shelters had no bedding. We slept directly on the ground, a comfortable sandy surface that was flat and dry. Because the place was close to a city, extra security measures were taken to guard against escape. Electrified barbed wire was all around. Police boxes and security posts were placed closely. The Liberation Army was vigilant around the clock. Cavalry patrolled the outskirts. When prisoners were sent to work, mounted guards ran back and forth to urge the procession to move faster. Any slowdown would provoke painful lashes.

Our task was to fortify the railroad bed south of the Bawang River Bridge. The roadbed was a twenty-meter high embankment. It had a slope of 45 degrees, too steep to withstand prolonged exposure to the weather, which would erode the embankment, endangering the safety of the trains. The plan was to reduce erosion by lowering the slope to 30 degrees and compact the soil. Our task was to pick up the soil, move it, and ram it. Because of the unmanageable terrain and the porous sandy soil, the job was quite difficult.

Civilian workers, road builders, and engineering corps had been unable to complete the job because of these obstacles. Only we reforming laborers could be driven hard enough to complete this daunting task. There was no suitable soil in the vicinity that could be packed firmly. To find clay soil, we had to go a long way to a heavily weeded place. Digging the soil from the densely rooted ground was arduous. The round trip over several hundred meters of rocky and rugged terrain was taxing and time-consuming. The work quota that the cadres had set was wishful thinking – totally impossible to meet, even with slave labor. Influenced by the evil axiom of "rather be high than low, rather be left than right," the quotas were always impossibly high. The cadres' only concern was the progress of the project. They paid no attention to the misery of the prisoners.

After many days of unbearable labor at Jining came the depth of winter. The cold winds came through Outer Mongolia one after another. The prisoner camp faced the gap in the mountain range. The swirls of icy cold wind often lifted the sand and pebbles into the air; you could not even open your eyes. The shelters were permeable to rain and wind, disrupting our sleep. By morning, our breath had frozen to the coverlet. Because our shelter, clothing, and nutrition were inadequate, and our work exhausting, our health was in serious jeopardy. Compared to the farm labor camp, the psychological burden here was much lighter. But the physical misery was much worse. It was hard to say which one was more intolerable.

Chapter 6 *Railroad Work in the West*

FOOD RATIONING

The severe winter was followed by a gentle spring. Although the piercing cold was gone, we now faced food rationing, a policy that threatened our health and life.

In the past, any important changes of policy were announced in a big meeting, handed down to the brigades and squads for study and discussion. Everyone was required to lay bare his position on the change and submit letters of assurance, determination, challenge, and acceptance. This time, all these procedures were bypassed. We were not told the reason for rationing, nor were we told how to cope with it.

We had meals three times a day on working days and twice on resting days. The meals consisted of corn, sorghum, or millet, and occasionally potato or another tuber. Every squad was given a small basin of salted cabbage soup. That was the only seasoning to help us swallow the coarse food. Because quantity was limited, consumption was closely monitored. Everyone took turns having a spoonful. In spite of the poor quality of the food, the prisoners were so hungry that the food gave them pleasure. Even the dregs in the bottom of the basin were consumed.

One day, a terrible thing happened. For the meal after work, some people had two bowls, but most had only one before the barrels of food were empty. Those who had not had enough carried the barrels to the pantry for more. But the service prisoners in the pantry told them there was no more food. Since I was a slow eater, I was one of those who had only one bowl of food. Angry over the food shortage, I followed the crowd to the pantry in search of hidden food, but we found none. The crowd reported it to the office. I did not go with them because I did not want to see the cadres on business matters. According to the people who went, the cadres listened to the report in silence.

At the end, they said, "Your report is noted. This was not a problem of the pantry. You should not disturb them anymore. Whoever does that again will be punished. How the problem arose, we will tell you later."

We thought this was an isolated case. I was so hungry that I could not sleep.

The next morning, based on the painful experience of the night before, we all rushed to fetch our share of food. Everyone filled his bowl.

Some tried to dish out the food with their bowls. Food was scattered all over the ground. Only a few got two bowls of food. But this time the situation was worse since the prisoners were hungrier and more desperate. This resulted in quarrels, which escalated into fistfights. In that chaos, I again had only one bowl.

After the monitors reported the chaos to the office, the captain arrived, along with his officers, in a rage. He ordered all of us to line up in formation. "What are you trying to do? Do you want to incite a riot? You are criminals. Do you know what double offense means? It means you are resisting reform, obstinately remaining the enemy of the people. You are on the road to extinction. 'Insufficiency finds its cause in contending for more. Surrender leads to plenty.' There is enough food if it is distributed evenly. Now all of you go to work. We will deal with the problem in the evening."

We all knew that we were under despotic rule. We also knew what a despotic ruler meant when the charge was "resistant to reform". Under this kind of coercion, no one dared to challenge it. We acquiesced. But most people still thought it was a temporary situation.

When we came back at noon, the commander, the officers, and some of the cadres were present. We were ordered to line up in formation. We fetched our share of food by taking turns. The second turn would not start until the first turn was complete. The person who was first in line in the first turn would be directed to the end of the line for the second turn. The prisoners were not allowed to scoop for themselves. The monitors served the food. This method avoided the commotion and chaos.

But when the distribution began there was another surprise. There was no solid food in the barrel, just porridge. When I got my share, I found that the porridge with some unpeeled potato granules was terribly diluted and unsalted. It was unpalatable. Our "bowls" were not even uniform in size. A "bowl" was just some sort of container that the prisoner had obtained on his own to hold food. It could be a porcelain enamel bowl or cup, an aluminum box, or even a small basin. Those from Zhejiang and Fujian provinces might even use bamboo or wooden utensils, also of varying sizes. At that meal, everyone fetched his share by taking turns. The circular movement worked like a merry-go-round. Everyone held a different kind of utensil, eating as he walked around, much like Taoist priests in a chanting ceremony. Nobody was amused.

This arrangement enabled each of us to eat three to four bowls of watery porridge, temporarily appeasing our hunger. But on the field, after working a short time, we had to urinate. After a short while, our hunger returned. We had insufficient energy to pick up, load, or ram. What seemed strange was that the usual supervisory visits of the commander, brigadiers, officers, and cadres discontinued that day. The work intensity slackened.

Supper that night was a replay of lunch. The increased frequency of urination disturbed our sleep, so that we were not ready the next morning to put in a good day's work. The same pattern was repeated for several days; discontent was mounting. Was the government intentionally starving us?

Finally, the supervisors announced that the food rationing was due to a natural disaster. The harvest for the whole country had failed and rationing was in place throughout the entire nation, not just for us. Everybody was asked to do his best to get through this difficult time.

I had not been paranoid except during the past few years. Having encountered so many deceitful schemes of the government, I no longer held any trust in it. The cadres did not announce the food rationing maybe because of their own conflicting feelings toward it. Their superiors wanted them to push us to speed up our work and finish the project on schedule; on the other hand, they did not give us enough food. Anyone with a conscience and reasoning ability would readily see that it was inhumane and senseless. But in order to reduce the discontent brewing among the prisoners, they had to bring this issue out into the open. Food rationing was a matter of life and death for the laborers.

From that point on, food rationing was enforced without equivocation. Our illusion that it would be temporary was dispelled. Hunger and despair overwhelmed our daily life. At least, the pressure for productivity slackened. We suffered terribly from the lack of food, and our work output markedly decreased. As a matter of fact, everyone was thinner and weaker. Some did not even have the energy to move around. I, who used to be satiated with a small intake, felt that this went beyond my sustainable threshold. The suffering of those larger in stature and younger could well be imagined.

One afternoon, a service prisoner carrying the porridge from the pantry stumbled. The barrel of porridge overturned, spilling all over. Many of the prisoners put both hands on the ground and scooped up spilled porridge. As the puddle of porridge spread over the ground, they could no longer effectively collect it, so they licked it off the ground, like dogs or hogs. As the sandy ground quickly absorbed the water content of the porridge, the "dogs and hogs" collected it and washed out the sand before eating. In a short while, the ground was as clear as if nothing had spilled. I was so hungry I almost wanted to get down on all fours to join them, but a shred of decency stopped me from becoming an animal. The events of that period made such an impression on me that in writing this section, the scenes of food rationing vividly replayed in my mind like on a television screen.

The reinforcement of the railroad bed south of the Bawang River Bridge was scheduled to be completed by summer. But we were so weakened by starvation that we didn't finish until late fall. One day, the office ordered all prisoners to get their shovels, hoes, flat sticks, and loaders ready to dig cabbage roots on the old country farm. They said that by mixing peeled cabbage roots into the porridge we could get some additional nourishment. The notice stirred up some excitement. All of us went in high spirits to the farm. When we finished digging, the roots filled many loaders. Happily, we carried them to the pantry.

After lunch, we all joined in to peel them. The peeled cabbage roots—crispy, tender, and palatable—tasted much like broccoli. That night, the porridge was more substantial and we all had an additional bowl. The field contained plenty of roots. We gradually returned from the brink of starvation. We were relieved to know that the government did not intend to starve us.

But the good days did not last long. The ground froze when winter came, making digging nearly impossible. Besides, the roots froze and were no longer edible. Meals reverted to the watery porridge. Our strenuous labor, combined with under nutrition, brought about more and more illness. Was there really a national food shortage? After six months of rationing, the number of debilitated prisoners increased dramatically.

Jining was at the gap of the peripheral mountain range. Cold winds came in one after another. The hunger-stricken prisoners had little energy to withstand the piercing cold. Many got colds and others had loose bowels. The latrines at the back of the shelters overflowed. The waste matter froze solidly into the ground. Once, after I had squatted and moved my bowels, I found that my feet had frozen to the ground from the accompanying urine. I could not move, so I took off my shoes and went barefoot to the tool room to get a heated spade to pry loose my shoes. This made me late for work, resulting in a reprimand. Other prisoners also suffered this undignified mishap.

For the cadres, prisoners' illnesses were a major annoyance. The more of us who were sick, the slower the progress. Therefore, sick leave was difficult to obtain. We were forced to work unless we were severely ill. Refusal to work was a serious offense. On many occasions, the office would have the squad monitor lead someone to the field. If he resisted, he would face punches and kicks then, and an ideological struggle in the evening. Those to whom sick leave was granted were treated shabbily. Folk remedies were the only medicines available. The excellent treatment of my foot injury had been a fortuitous exception.

Those with serious illnesses were transferred out immediately. Where they were sent, nobody knew; not one of them ever returned. Under the strict policy that prohibited people from getting close, which was considered a sign of clique formation, there was no chance to make friends. Since nobody had the time or energy to take care of himself, no one cared what happened to the next person. I was told that most of those transferred died later, but what really happened remained a mystery.

55 KILOMETERS

With weak and infirm laborers, the railroad project progressed slowly. Very little got done after the Spring Festival. Except for a small number left behind to handle the wrap-up, most of us were moved westward to build the Baotou-Baiyun Ebo Railroad. High quality coal and iron ore had been discovered in Baiyun Ebo. The exploration and mining work had already begun. The rail line would carry the coal and iron ore to Baotou for the iron and steel industry there.

About a thousand prisoners were being moved. We traveled from Jining to Baotou by train. From Baotou, we were taken by truck to "55 Kilometers," the temporary name for a desolate spot on the line 55 kilometers from Baotou, where a station was planned.

A cavalry regiment escorted our procession. Its grandeur and gallantry attracted many a passerby's eye. The first part of the trip was on the highway. After the highway ended, the truck went along a sandy riverbed, a seasonal artery that had water during the summer and fall. The riverbed was essentially made of rocks. Although the trucks did not get stuck, they frequently skidded. We encountered two steep hills. The trucks would not be able to climb over them. We all had to get out and push the trucks while the engines were running. We got back on board again at the top of the hill. The fully loaded trucks swayed as they rolled down the hill. The prisoners who sat atop the luggage dangerously stuck out of the truck above the railings. As the trucks swayed to and fro, we were seized with panic.

At "55 Km," we were to work on the railroad bedding, just like we had at Jining. In Jining, we worked with earth, but here it was with rocks. At first, I thought the rail bed would be laid on top of the riverbed because only the riverbed was flat. There were hills on both sides of the river. But the plan was to create a flat base on one side of the river through the mountain pass by cutting down some of the rocks on the slope to fill in the ditches below. At the beginning, the cutting was on the surface of the hill where the rocks were eroded and porous. Later, the large and solid rocks had to be blasted away with gunpowder. The rocks usually fell to where they were needed, and since we were dealing with rocks rather than earth, there was no need for ramming. So the work at "55 Km" was not as exhausting as at Jining.

The work rating system could credit you with the block you cut and filled. Since filling occurred automatically by gravity, you got double credit. The supervisors of the brigade and the cadres did not pressure us too much. To us weak, poorly nourished prison laborers, the easier work was a great blessing.

Meanwhile, the prisoners faced a new problem. Walking over sharp rocks all day, we quickly wore out the soles of our shoes. A new pair of shoes hardly lasted a week. I had one pair of old shoes. After a few days of labor, my soles ruptured. To cope with this situation, the office distributed a bunch of cloth shoes from a nearby town. But cloth shoes wore out even faster. We tried all kinds of makeshift remedies. Some tied the worn-out soles onto the newer shoes. Still others put a piece of wood or sheet metal inside the shoe to cover the hole in the sole. Others sewed a piece of cloth on their socks. But the best method was to apply some asphalt onto the soles, then stomp on the sand and granulated stone. After the soles cooled off, they became strong and resistant to abrasion. Since we were in an area of construction, stone, sand, and asphalt were plentiful. We solved the shoe problem!

Our padded tops and pants had been issued almost two years ago. Through long wear, they were extremely ragged and patched, making us look like vagabonds. My clothes were badly frayed. My top had two holes on the shoulders and my trousers had even more holes. In several places, they were on the verge of falling apart. I had to tie up the holes with twine.

Because the prisoners' clothes were in such an intolerable condition, the office notified us that a new batch of padded tops and pants would soon be distributed. The commander specifically noted that there might not be enough for everyone, so priority would be given to those whose clothes were the most ragged. Those whose clothes were not as worn out would be given their allotment next time. He urged the prisoners to show their generosity by conceding rather than fighting. His announcement only led the prisoners to secretly tear up their halfway decent clothes. In order not to let the others see what they were doing, it was done late at night or in the toilet. They did so because they believed that there would not be another distribution in the foreseeable future.

The following afternoon after work, an assembly was called to distribute the new clothes. The brigadiers, the officers, and the cadres were all present. They inspected everybody's clothes and distributed a new set to those wearing the most ragged clothes.   Only ten prisoners received a set of new clothes. The brigadier general reassured them that they would soon be given some new clothes. In the meantime, they were allowed to pick up another suit from the discarded pile or repair what they were wearing. This arrangement did little to soothe their discontent.

My clothes had been among the most ragged, so I was among the first to get a new set. After this distribution, I submitted a suggestion to the office, "During this distribution of clothes, priority was given according to the degree of raggedness of the old suits. Those whose clothes were the most ragged were the first to receive new ones. Many people, lest theirs were not ragged enough, secretly tore up their reasonably good clothes in order to improve their chances of getting new ones. I suggest that in future distributions, new suits be given first to those whose old suits were best cared for. Those with ragged ones will be left for last. If the supply is insufficient, those who did not get new ones will be given a suit from the discards. The office will provide needles, thread, scissors, and cloth pieces for mending."

The office liked the idea and called a meeting to announce it. It was well-received among the prisoners. After that everyone took good care of his suit. The clothing situation in the brigade showed a marked improvement.

The cadres commented, "After all, he is a college graduate. He has good ideas." Since my arrest, being a college graduate had often been a reason for censure and ridicule. Only this time had it turned out to be a commendable achievement.

Not long after that, they appointed me as the monitor for learning and communication. My duties as communicator were to handle prisoners' mail, parcels, and remittances; to relay orders and notices from the office; and to do the paperwork for the office, such as making statistical reports or copying documents. The job was not very strenuous or complex, but because of that post, my labor assignments were reduced. In the meantime, I was no longer the target of the scoundrels among the prisoners. My affinity with the cadres induced some fear and respect among the other prisoners; on the other hand, life was not as simple as before. Many cast an envious eye upon my position. They thought that with less physical work, I had the opportunity to impress the cadres, which could pave the way to reducing my penalty. By nature, I do not like too much responsibility and am loath to deal with people in an official capacity, but there was no way for me to decline this plum of an assignment. I had made the suggestion about the clothes in the interest of all the prisoners; little did I expect this "promotion" for myself.

GROUP EVALUATION

Since we had been at "55 Km," many had fallen ill from malnutrition, requiring their transfer to the sick quarters. One evening, all squad monitors were called to a meeting. They brought back a strange order. All squads were required to grade the physical capacity of their members: A = strong, B = average, and C = weak. The grading process had three parts: self-appraisal, group evaluation, and office approval. We were not told the reason for the grading. Some thought more taxing jobs needed stronger personnel to carry them out. Others thought special consideration would be given to the old and infirm, lightening their workload. Still others thought the whole group was to be reorganized for new deployment. I knew from past experience that this procedure would have a major effect on our lives. Anything not fully disclosed usually made our life worse.

The grading sessions took place that night. No one knew whether a high or low grade was more beneficial.

As the monitor for learning, I said, "Since nobody wants to be the first, maybe the monitor for labor and I should start to offer our appraisals. I appraise myself as category B."

Then I turned toward the monitor for labor, "How about you?"

After a pause, he asserted, "I appraise myself as A."

Since the monitor for labor was the strongest and highest performing person in the group, his claim of category A was indisputable. Then I asked the group whether they would like to make the group evaluation right after each self-appraisal or if they preferred to wait for all the self-appraisals to be done first. The group could not make up its mind, so I suggested that we complete the self-appraisals first, and then go on to make the group evaluations. My suggestion won consensus. By the time we were about to start the self-appraisals, the bedtime bell rang and the meeting was adjourned.

The grading continued the following evening. The self-appraisals went rather smoothly, but the group evaluation less so. Since nobody knew whether an A or a C was the better grade, there seemed no reason to argue over grades. But when an appraisal was obviously inaccurate, the arguing began; we did not get through half the list in two and a half hours, so we needed a third evening to finish.

Two days after the grades were submitted, the authorities called a meeting to announce, "It has been more than a year since food rationing was put into effect. Thanks to the flawless government policy and your law-abiding spirit, things have gone smoothly. But there are still a small number who are resistant to reform and have grumbled privately, spreading the seeds of discontent. We are taking this opportunity to warn them. You eels in the mud could never raise a big wave. If you do not reform, you will be severely punished. For the past year or so, you each have been eating equal portions. We now know how to make the system fairer. To let the stronger, who perform well, eat the same amount as the weaker, who do less work, is unfair. We asked you to grade your physical capacities for the purpose of breaking this superficial evenhandedness. From now on, rations are in accordance with physical capacity. Food will be provided in buns of sorghum or corn. Category A gets a ration of four buns, Category B, three buns, and Category C, two buns. Each squad will be provided with two kegs of boiled water per meal. All monitors are required to make a list of each member and his grade. The number of people in each category should also be noted. Copies are to be filed with the office and the pantry. At mealtime, the pantry will provide the exact number of buns to the monitors, who in turn will distribute them to the members according to their ration. Should there be any unlawful acts, quarrels, or other troubles, the monitor will immediately report the offenders for punishment."

The announcement produced a commotion among the prisoners. Nobody had expected the grading to be related to food distribution. The next day, the new rationing system was put into practice. Squad monitors went to the pantry to pick up the provisions for their group. The pantry distributed the exact number of buns according to the list. Each bun was the size of a goose egg but hollow in the center. The buns were bell-shaped, which made them look bigger and were easier to cook. Each monitor took buns back to his squad and distributed them to the members according to grade. He then sent two members to pick up the kegs of boiled water, barely sufficient for each person to have a cupful. The scarcity of water, which had to be brought in by truck from far away, resulted in the restriction of drinking water and the elimination of porridge. Water was so scarce that each squad was given only two basins of water each morning for face washing. No water was supplied for any other use. Full of filth, the shelters were permeated by an offensive odor. The water shortage was not relieved until spring, when the creek at the foot of the mountain began to melt.

My allotment of three buns offered me the same sustenance as the bowls of porridge. Since less water meant less urinating, I slept better. Those on A rations were better off than before, but for those on C rations, the two hollow buns, which could be finished in a few bites, did not leave them even half full. Most of the laborers on C rations lost considerable muscle mass and also experienced psychological deterioration. They became so ill they had to be transferred to sick quarters. Some died before they could be transferred.

39 KILOMETERS

Now summer had arrived. After a few rainfalls, clear water gushed forth from the creek running through the valley. Wildflowers bloomed along both sides of the creek. We dug many pits along the way to collect water for laundering and bathing. The pristine water from the creek was refreshing to drink. Our long thirst was over.

By that time, the construction work at "55 Km" was nearly complete. The flat ground where our shelters stood was to be the site of the station. Most of the prisoners had to be transferred to another workplace to make way for the ensuing construction. Only a small number of people were left for winding up the job.

The new workplace was a wild no-man's-land called "39 Km", also named after its distance from Baotou. The shelters were set on a piece of flat land. The roadbed for the main line was already done. Our work was to build the bed for a two-kilometer fork. This time we were working with earth, not rock. Working with earth was much more strenuous than working with rocks. Furthermore, since the bed was built at an elevation, the earth had to be carried uphill.

During this period, I came to know prisoner Xu, a former bank employee in Shanghai. Xu and I were in the same brigade but different squads. Oftentimes after work, we got together and talked about the manners, customs, and past events of Shanghai. Strong and big in stature, he was on A rations. Due to a covert report accusing him of indolence and negligence, his ration was cut to B, which was clearly insufficient. So he made a direct appeal to the commander, who told him that reinstatement was possible if he could prove himself through excellent performance.

He was elated by this promise and began to work with extra zeal. Since his workplace was not far from mine, we could generally see each other on the field. When I did not see him at work for two or three days, I thought he must have fallen sick. But when I asked some of his colleagues, I was startled to learn that he had died. Only a few days ago, he had looked very normal and was working at a good pace with his loader. How could his death be that sudden? Had he had an accident?

After work, I went to the clinic to ask the doctor, who told me that Xu had been working so hard that he had a fatal heart attack on the field.

Xu was a good-hearted and straightforward intellectual. He was one of my friends, one of my only friends. I was deeply saddened to lose him, but I realized that his quick death had spared him the prolonged torment of death by starvation or illness.

The soil for the bed was scooped from 50 meters away. We were allowed to dig two meters deep. After that, the digging area had to be extended. The earth was sandy, porous, and loose—not hard to scoop. However, there were many roots that had to be removed; otherwise they would decay and weaken the roadbed. The roots that were picked out were thrown back into the pits from which the earth had been taken. The big ones were the diameter of a finger; the small ones the diameter of a chopstick. At first, nobody knew what kind of roots they were. Then one of the prisoners realized it was licorices, a sweet herb popular in Chinese medicine. Licorices became our windfall confection, popular with all the prisoners. Some sucked or chewed it; others soaked it in water to make licorices "tea."

But after a week, some found that their face or limbs had swelled up; some suffered a swelling of their penis. Only my fingers and toes became swollen. It was bad enough, but it could have been worse. The doctor told us that licorices had to be cured first; otherwise, it would cause swelling. When the prisoners were on the field, the supervisors searched the shelters and confiscated all the licorices. In the meantime, they asked the herbal shops in town to send trucks and remove all the licorice roots from the field. Eating licorice was prohibited. Once we stopped licorice, the swelling disappeared within a few days. Why didn't they let us cure the licorice so that we could safely enjoy it?

A few months after we had started working at "39 km," a new group of prisoners joined us. This influx of new prisoners was somewhat stressful because of our limited shelter, food, water, and fuel. Fortunately, there were not too many of them, so it was not difficult to place them into different squads. The person who joined our squad was from the farms in northern Jiangsu Province. Because I had been there, his arrival interested me. According to him, last summer a typhoon had destroyed all the cotton fields, trenches, and shelters, so all the prisoners had to be redeployed.

Naturally, I asked, "Do you know what became of the insurrection gang case from about two years ago?"

"The case came to a close six months after you left."

"What was the outcome?"

"Seven or eight people were executed. Many of the others were given long sentences.

"Do you remember a certain Mr. Fei? Was he executed?"

"Was he a college graduate of short stature?"

"Yes, that's the one. He was my townsman."

"He was executed. He was the leader."

That is what I had expected. Mr. Fei must have known that "to strive for lenient disposition" was futile. He didn't involve any innocent people since he would have been executed regardless. Had he implicated me, I might have joined him on the execution field. I would have been surprised if he was not executed. The Communists in handling such cases definitely would not be merciful or hesitant. Otherwise, how could there be so many wrongful prosecutions and deaths during the purge and oppression sessions? The case had been weighing on my mind for some time. Knowing how the case ended was a big relief.

In the meantime, I had an agonizing thought. Under Communism, a sense of insecurity or dread overflowed into everyone's mind, except those in power and, perhaps, certain political opportunists. Even if you were prudent and careful in every respect, you still could not escape unexpected blows. A wrong word, a wrong letter, or a wrong friend, all could lead you to prison or death. The death of Fei not only opened an old wound, it also compounded my fears. As a political prisoner under this regime, my situation could be as dreadful as those executed. But there was no way for me to flee from this predicament. I still had to struggle for my existence. The closure of the insurrection case relieved me from possible involvement, but the news of executions caused me much pain.

HANGMAN'S PASS

The engineering work at "39 Km" was relatively simple; we completed it in a few months. Our group was dispatched to Xishanzui (literally, the mouth of the western mountains) on the Baotou-Lanzhou Railway. The place was more than a hundred kilometers southeast of Baotou. We started out in trucks but traveled the last fifty kilometers by foot, with our backpacks sent on by truck. With a one-hour lunch break, we arrived at our destination at five. Most of us, including me, had worn-out shoes and blistered feet.

The first things upon arrival were group and shelter assignments. The squad I was assigned to had a few middle-aged Mongolians. One of them had his bedding right next to mine. A strong, uncultured man, he was unkempt and dirty. He wore sheepskin jacket and sheepskin trousers with no underwear. The fur of the sheepskin had already turned ashen and stiff. His body odor made those around him swoon. Despite appearances, he was fair and reasonable. Frank and outspoken, he spoke fluent Mandarin. During our conversations, I inquired about Mongolian customs. The Mongolians frequently expressed bitterness against the Communist regime. Surprisingly, these remarks never resulted in punishment. For some reason the authorities were lenient with the Mongolians.

Xishanzui was the entry point of the mountain pass of Daqing Shan (the Great Green Range) that lay between Baotou and Yinchuan. With the sinister name of Hangman's Pass, it meandered along the cliffs on both sides of the gorge. The pass was lushly clothed with luxuriant forests and thickets. The strangely-shaped rocks looked like various animals. Rapid streams running through the glacier deposit in the valley often burst into scattered clear ponds. Flowers in different colors were everywhere. One of them had the shape of a traditional Chinese palace lantern. This breathtaking scene was more magnificent than Hangzhou's Nine Streams and Eighteen Brooks, and Beijing's Cherry Creek of Fragrant Hill. Hangman's Pass, with its many forks, extended more than a hundred kilometers. It was the hideout of bandits and the Chinese armed forces were powerless to pursue them.

The type of work at "39 Km" was somewhat different from previous assignments. This time, we had to crush rocks into small pieces approximately five centimeters in diameter using steel hammers. The job was less taxing than the previous one, but, of course, there was the work quota, which had been set rather high. The weaklings still had to work long hours to meet it. I was an average worker; it was not too difficult for me to meet the quota. Competitions to be the most productive became a regular occurrence. As the cadres liked to say, "Labor must be full of vitality and burn with ardor." But behind that vitality and burning ardor was the exhausted flesh and blood of the prisoners. As the monitor of

Chapter 6 *Railroad Work in the West*

learning, I had to set a good example as a productive worker.

A month later, in the heart of summer, the heat was intolerable. The ground was so hot that it burned my feet as the heat traveled right through the soles of my shoes. Luckily, my work area was in the shady pass surrounded by steep hills and dense forests, where I was protected from the heat. The clear water creeks and the flowers and plants gave me pleasure. The working conditions at "39 Km," except for the insufficient food supply, were the best during my years of forced labor.

But, as usual, the good days did not last long. The next disaster was a flu epidemic. For a normal community, flu is usually not a calamity. But in a labor camp, the crowded conditions and the lack of doctors and medicine quickly turned a few isolated cases into an epidemic. Over half the members of my squad, including myself, came down with the flu. Unless critically ill, we were forced to work. I developed a high fever that made me unconscious. The doctor gave me medicine, but it didn't work. He didn't tell me the name of the medicine and it was taboo to ask. It might even have been a placebo. After many days of lethargy, I improved and my fever broke. I made it through that deadly illness, but I was emaciated and my hair had fallen out. My hair never grew back. Despite my weakened condition, I still had to meet the work quota. On the other hand, I was lucky enough to get well and was not sent to sick quarters. Many others were sent, never to be seen again.

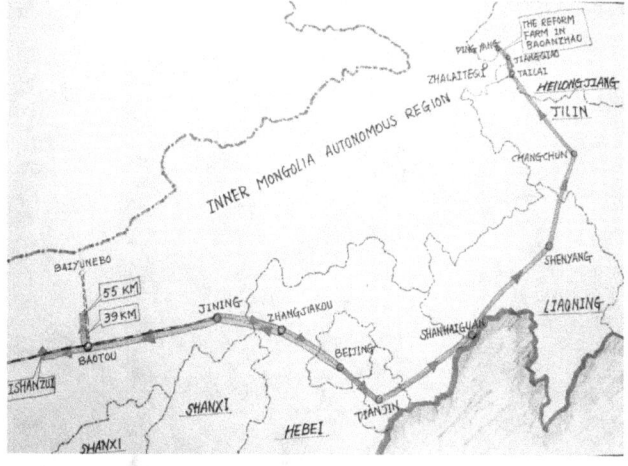

CHAPTER 7

FARMING IN BAOANZHAO, INNER MONGOLIA

Chapter 7 *Farming in Baoanzhao, Inner Mongolia*

REPAIR DRY DAM

Remarkably, we had a five-day rest period during the Spring Festival. This occurred at the completion of our assignment, which enhanced the cheerful atmosphere of the Festival. The weather was sunny and warm. In the big courtyard, some of us were mending and patching our clothes, others were reading or playing chess, and still others were casually socializing. The tranquility and leisure dispelled our misery temporarily. Then we were ordered to depart.

Last spring when we had arrived in Xishanzui, the railroad bedding was already complete, but more crushed stone needed to be placed in between the logs. Furthermore, the rails had not yet been set in place. At the time of our departure, the rails extended from Baotou to an outpost of Yinchuan, the midpoint of the Baotou-Lanzhou Railway. This time, we boarded a train at a small station a little south of Xishanzui. Again, we traveled in an old freight car, but this time the allotted space was even more generous than before—enough room for us to lie down. Before boarding, everyone was given a few salted buns—palatable if one were hungry enough. En route, we had to exercise restraint and not eat too much too soon or we would not have enough for the rest of the journey.

Our slow special dispatch could only run between the scheduled trains. We had long stops at almost every station. Drinking water was supplied twice a day; the toilet barrel was emptied once a day. Since we already had our provisions, the bustle of serving meals was avoided. This was a good solution the cadres came up with from their experience.

After two nights and one day, the temperature dropped steadily because, after Beijing and Tianjin, the train turned northward beyond the Shanhaiguan. Our final destination, the Baoanzhao Farm was a few hundred kilometers north of that pass. The metal freight car lost heat rather quickly, becoming very chilly. At the break of dawn, we arrived at the town of Pingyang of Heilongjiang Province.

It was getting lighter, but the sun was not yet out—the coldest moment of the day. We walked one kilometer to a school and had a breakfast of millet congee with salted cabbage. My fingers were numb from the cold. I could not even hold my chopsticks but somehow managed to eat one bowl of the hot congee.

After breakfast we walked 20 kilometers in four hours, arriving at our new assignment—the second battalion of the Baoanzhao Farm. Trucks sent by the farm brought our luggage. The so-called farm was simply a prison on a grand scale. The prisoners who were already there were working on some major improvements, such as building roads or houses, levelling the ground, and draining ditches. They were preparing the land for farming. Up to that moment, not a single crop had been planted. Before we arrived, the cadres had told us that the farm would supply staples and other foods in abundance—a rosy picture, a fantasy.

On arrival, we were assigned dorms. The dorms consisted of rows of south-oriented adobe huts. There were twenty rows of huts. Each row had eight huts, with a separate entrance for every four units. Each hut had two brick beds, each sleeping six, that were heated by fire. In addition, there was the pantry, warehouse, office, and clinic. A square wall surrounded the yard. Armed guards were positioned at each corner. It took us a full afternoon to clean the dorms, seal off the doors and windows, and collect hay for heating the beds.

Assignments were given that very evening. Our job was to break up the ice and drain the ditch. But the work site was far from our huts. Before we left for work the following morning, we were given our lunch and tools. We were closely watched en route and were under armed surveillance while we worked. At lunch, everyone took out his wrapped buns. Still on B ration, I had three hollow goose-egg-sized buns with no drink. Although thirsty, the advantage was that I urinated less often. In the severe cold, taking off my gloves and unbuttoning my trousers would be a painful maneuver.

Winter in the north was marginally bearable if there were no high winds. Cold winds were debilitating for poorly nourished laborers. Our resistance to illness was low, and many of us fell sick. The clinic was very strict about issuing certificates of sickness. Sick leave was even more difficult to obtain. I once suffered a severe cold with headaches and a high fever, but my request for leave was denied. I was compelled to go to the field and work the whole day. At the end of the day, I stumbled back to my bed and collapsed. But I would not let them beat me into total submission; I would live through the ordeal of the labor camps and see brighter days.

Baoanzhao Farm was fifty kilometers south of the City of Qiqihaer of Heilongjiang Province, the intersection of Jiangqiao County of Heilongjiang and Zhalaite Qi of Inner Mongolia. Being in the sub-frigid zone, it had a very long winter. From mid-March to mid-April, temperatures were below freezing in the morning and evening but above freezing around noon. There was frost until late April. Trees and flowers began to bud in mid-May. During the vibrant spring, we were called to a new task.

Our new job was to raise and fortify a dry dam. The administration's utilization of prisoners' labor was disorganized and impulsive. Totally unprepared, I packed my belongings and followed the crowd to the new site, the Brigade of Hings, located near the dam. We would be housed in little grass huts that were damp and musty, with no windows. Upon arrival, we all went out for hay to cover the moist floor. Then we unpacked our luggage and set up the bedding. We would be here for some time.

Originally, the dam was built by prisoners to guard against possible flooding of the Chuoer River, a branch of the Nenjiang River. The dam was five meters high, five meters wide at the base, and two meter wide at the top. Because neither the height nor the width was sufficient, the last inundation of rain overflowed the dam, submerging a vast piece of farmland and crops. The rain had also created some cracks in the dam. Our task was to make the dam higher and wider, and to patch the cracks.

We were required to take earth only from within fifty meters of the dam. When the earth piled up, it was necessary to ram it. Because we had to move the earth uphill, the job was extremely exhausting. Filling the cracks was even more difficult because the torrential rains had carved deep pits which had accumulated with water. We had to remove all the water from the pits before the cracks could be filled. Because of the tremendous amount of earth required for the project, the location for dredging extended farther and farther.

The intensity of the work rose steeply. Prisoners with marginal food intake had no way of fulfilling the high quota. Work hours were extended. We had to get up before dawn, go to work in the dark, and return in the dark. Not counting lunch in the field, we worked over ten hours a day. Under these conditions, many prisoners on B or C rations became ill and were sent to the quarters for the sick, thus reducing the number of workers. My squad of 24 was reduced to less than ten. To make matters worse, the buns actually shrunk in size, so the remaining workers had to work harder and eat less.

It was summer. Weeds bloomed with vitality at the worksite and around the huts. We found amaranth and alfalfa, both edibles. During lunch break or after work, we went all out digging up these plants and boiled them in washbasins. Since there was an abundance of dry branches and hay, there was no shortage of fuel. Since the buns did not fill me up, I also cooked some amaranth and alfalfa to eat. They were somewhat bitter but nevertheless palatable. When cooked with salt stolen from the pantry, it was quite tasty.

One day someone dug up a reddish tuberous root. Those who tried it said it was sweet and tender. From my earlier experiences at camp, I learned to avoid novel endeavors; therefore, I stayed away from this mystery tuber, which turned out to be a good move. It turned out to cause abdominal pain and vomiting. One man even died from it. Later, we were told that the tuber was extremely toxic, that its Chinese name meant "wolfish venom." Another plant that grew near water and looked like celery with red tips and a strong odor was also poisonous. I never tried it since I didn't like its smell. The eating of wild plants prevailed in camp because we were so hungry. But I preferred hunger to the unknown perils of wild plants.

The compulsory learning sessions after a day of heavy toil compounded our exhaustion. One day after work, a battalion meeting was called to speed up the pace of our work. We were ordered to complete the project before the rainy season. Although the battalion meeting lasted deep into the night, we were ordered to hold group discussions in each squad. Every individual was required to lay bare his position, offer challenges and assurances of cooperation, and encourage others' acceptance. It was a tedious process. We were so tired that we were not making any progress. I was so dizzy from sleep deprivation that I could no longer even record the comments. So, I called off the meeting and let everyone retire before the official order for adjournment. Everyone was happy and went to bed. Only the monitor for labor stayed up and said nothing. I thought he was meditating and did not bother to ask why. The next evening the office called me in.

"When did your squad go to bed last night?" the counselor asked.

"It was very late, long after lights-out," I replied, realizing that probably the labor monitor had turned me in.

"Were the discussions complete? Were the assurance papers and the challenge and acceptance papers drafted? Did the office order you to end the session early?" he asked.

"Discussions had completed. The assurance and the challenge and acceptance papers were pending," I answered.

"Someone reported that you ordered your squad to go to bed when other squads were still at the height of their discussions. Is that true?"

"I saw that all the members were extremely tired and unable to complete the task properly. I asked them to go to bed so that they could get up early in the morning for work." In an impasse, I tried to sidestep his question.

"Extremely tired? Was it only your squad that was tired? Other squads were not tired? You are the education monitor. How could you use tiredness as an excuse for breaking the rules for studying? You went to bed without permission before finishing the task and told your members to do the same. You committed a breach and made others follow in your inappropriate footsteps. What kind of attitude does this show toward reform? I have come across some unfavorable reports about you that said you do not grasp learning, you procrastinate, and are slow. I did not believe the reports, but now they have been proven true. You lag behind ideologically. You are not interested in striving for a better disposition. There are many others in your group who want to get ahead. Everything you did was reported. We will quickly find another person to take your place as education monitor. Write and submit a self-criticism. Do a good job. If you do not clearly show repentance, we will have to punish you."

I had no defense for my actions. In a downcast mood, I went back to my hut. I did not mind no longer being the education monitor. I would be spared frequent contacts with the officers, whose dogma and brainwashing I found distasteful. However, I worried that the case might not close that easily.

Two days later, the counselor came to our squad. He reprimanded me for my mistake and declared that I was discharged as education monitor. He appointed another person in my place. About a week later, the trouble I was expecting sprang up. Someone went to the office and reported me for being idle and slothful. They said that I dawdled during work, urinated frequently, filled the baskets meagerly, and moved the loads too slowly. When I was called into the office, the brigadier general read me all the reports and asked me whether they were true. I denied them and told him that my performance matched my B status. I could not compare with the A prisoners, but I was doing my best.

The brigadier exposed my statement by saying that if I had done my best, why was there no similar reports on others. He asked me to prove that I was performing well. Finally he warned me that if I did not improve my performance, he would have to lower my ration to C. At that point, he signaled for me to leave. He did not ask me to write any statements. I went back to the squad feeling most unhappily. First I was blamed for not handling the education well, and then I was accused of inadequate work performance. The downgrading of the rations was a real threat. I knew all too well how poorly the C group fared. All I could do was put forth a superhuman effort for these taskmasters. Fortunately, my rations were not downgraded and I did not fall down dead from a heart attack like my friend Xu.

BIG NEW FARM

It was midsummer and we had been working on the dam fortification project for two months. The Chuoer River would soon be inundated with rain. Cadres pressured us to go to all lengths to meet the deadline. But the cadres were still not satisfied and criticized us for not putting forth our best effort. At that time, the battalion commander was removed for ineffective administration and for lagging ideologically.

One day after work, the new commander called a meeting to give us his initial scolding. The meeting was held in a rustic setting near the dam. A temporary platform was set up at one end of the grounds, dimly lit by a few lanterns. Flashlights around the field indicated the presence of armed guards. The speech was a repeat of the same old clichés. He complained that the prisoners' work lacked intensity and their achievements fell behind requirements. He demanded that the fortification work be completed before the imminent rising of the water level. He also announced that in the future, meetings for competition, punishment, and commendation would be held to reward the good workers and penalize the idle. Gesticulating wildly and yelling at the top of his lungs, his voice shook the loudspeakers and pierced our ears. He was full of threats but empty of new ideas. Under the light of the lanterns, he looked ghastly and ghostly. His endless talk was primarily for the consumption of his superiors. He rattled on until midnight, making sure that we would be too tired in the morning to work productively.

The next day, the new commander came to the field with his entourage, carrying a stick. When he saw workers with heavy loads walking slowly, he railed against them and flogged them. In the dredging area, when the loaders did not fill the baskets to the top, he packed the earth firm and scooped more into the baskets until the soil was about twenty centimeters above the edge. Such a full load weighed at least sixty kilograms, exceeding our capacity. The strong, young workers tried to carry this heavy load, but they had to frequently put the basket down and rest. On the top of the dam, he complained that the ramming team was not quick enough and did not compact the earth with sufficient force, so he flogged them, too.

His visits to the field were frequent and foul. Hated and feared, he was labeled the Crazy Commander by the prisoners. Actually, he was not really crazy or sadistic, he was only acting. Even when he flogged us, he did not hit us too hard. Because his predecessor had been fired for being ineffectual at squeezing more work out of the prisoners, the Crazy Commander had to show a bit of cruelty and intimidation to stay on the job.

His case reminded me of another time in northern Jiangsu Province. While I was there, the brigadier general was particularly benevolent and reasonable. He understood the painful situation of the prisoners. He covertly took care of them. The idiots among the prisoners who could not visualize the prevailing political climate showed their appreciation by nicknaming him the Buddha Brigadier. This affectionate title became widely known. After a while, he suddenly changed his posture, becoming very strict in all respects; sometimes even absurdly cruel, such as denying leave for serious illness. His 180-degree change surprised everyone. Later, we found out that after the office found out about his nickname of Buddha Brigadier, he was severely reprimanded for his indulgence and lack of a firm political stand. He went from one extreme to the other, partly to correct his past "mistakes," and partly to take revenge on the prisoners who had gotten him in trouble. The affectionate but careless nickname not only hurt him but adversely affected all of us. The prisoners, upon learning the truth, took the harsh treatment stoically.

FLOOD SEASON

The fortification job had to be finished before the water level rose. The seasonal flood of the Chuoer River had two sources, the melted snow from the mountainous Xin'anling area and the seasonal rains.

One day at noon in early August, the Flood Control Office in the area sent a notice to the field, reporting that telephone calls from upstream warned that the flood would reach our spot that very day. In the distance, I saw nothing. Two hours later, someone shouted, "The flood is coming." Looking westward, I saw nothing at first. After a while, I saw a glimmering white line approaching. Not until it moved very close did I recognize that the glittering white line was the reflection of the water spray. The overflow was not as violent and torrential as I had imagined. It was just a body of water flowing over the ground, about half a meter deep, pushing gently eastward. Bushes and mounds of dirt remained above the water. But considering the vast land between the river and the dam, the volume of water was considerable.

That very afternoon, an order was issued. "Because the project did not meet the deadline, the flood reached here before the work was completed. We are ordering an emergency measure. All workers will be divided into two shifts, working around the clock, concentrating on the vulnerable spots of the dam."

The new arrangement started immediately. Those assigned to day duty went back to the shelters, leaving those on the late shift to continue their work. I was on the day shift so I left for the day.

When I came back the next morning, I was shocked by what I saw. The water had nearly reached the top of the dam. On the other side of the dam was a vast expanse of water. Except for a few branches of big trees, everything else was immersed.

I was assigned to block the gaps at the base of the dam. At first, we tried to pack more earth into a hole. But the gush of water was so intense that the earth was flushed away as soon as I poured it down the hole. We then plugged up the hole with a large number of bags filled with withered grass, leaves and branches. This was the right solution. It took 48 hours for the two teams to complete the job. Unfortunately, a big storm followed. The water level continued to rise, and some of the bags floated up. The water level was only half a meter below the top of the dike. This was an emergency requiring extreme measures. The supervisors ordered all prisoners, regardless of their shift, to work day and night. They also called up other labor forces in the area to come to our aid.

During the day the temperature was around 30 C° (86 F°); at night, it fell to 15 C° (59 F°). Working in this relatively cool place was advantageous because we didn't perspire too much. But during storms, the temperature could be frigid. At the time of the flood, we hit such a cold spell. Drenched with rain, workers in the field trembled from the severe cold. I had been used to the cold since childhood but still felt that working in these cold, wet conditions was unbearable. In the murky night under the thunderclouds, we had trouble seeing. The only lights we had were the few lanterns on top of the dam. The flashlights held by the armed guards flashed intermittently. In the darkness, the bushes and trees beckoned as hideouts; it was an ideal time to run away. But where could one run when the whole country was but one giant prison? Hungry and cold, a feeble and sickly person would only starve or freeze to death if he escaped.

We fought all night to save the dam from bursting and the field from flooding. At dawn, the rain stopped and the clouds dispersed. The east glowed from the rising sun. The water level subsided. The office upstream sent out information that the crest of the tide had passed. The crisis was over. We were extremely hungry and thirsty. Soon buns and boiled water were sent to the field. In order to reward us for our toil and hardship, rationing was waived on this occasion. Satiated with food and drink, everyone felt more comfortable. The day turned a little warmer. Compared with the night before, it felt like another world.

Work continued after our meal. By noon, the water level dropped another meter. The threat to the dam subsided further. The day shift, having worked continuously for over thirty hours, was sent back to the shelters. After this crisis, many prisoners fell ill. I was lucky to be spared. One person in our squad, who had been sick before the crisis, was denied sick leave on grounds of pretense. The office accused him of feigning illness. He was forced to go back to work. After a few days of intensive work, he got worse. He moaned all night and disturbed our sleep. The next morning, when everyone else got up, he was still in bed. He did not respond when the squad monitor went to rouse him. He was dead. I grieved deeply for his death. His was a fate that we all might have shared.

The danger of flooding was over. The night shift was discontinued. Life and work returned to its earlier pace. In another few days, all the water receded back to the river. Having been attacked by the current, the base of the dam had scattered pits and holes.

Except for a small detachment assigned to repair these defects, all the other laborers were deployed to a new task—plowing the barren land for rice fields. The Farm Commission had imported a few powerful tractors called Stalin-80s from the Soviet Union. A squad of twenty people was assigned to each tractor. Our job was to follow the tractors, turning the furrow slices over and flattening them. The job sounded simple, but because the virgin grassland was full of tangled roots like a loofah gourd, the clods of earth would not turn over until they were cut into pieces with sharp instruments. On bumpy land where the tractor turned, the slices were badly tangled and even more difficult to flatten. No matter how hard we worked, we couldn't keep up with the tractor. The only way to complete the task was to continue our work long after the tractor stopped. It was a totally exhausting day.

Underfed and overworked, our health continued to decline. The number of sick and dead continued to mount. As a stop-gap measure, the office dried up some newly acquired soybean pods and sunflower seed shells and ground them into powder. They mixed the powder with corn flour for our buns. The mixture not only made the buns more substantial but infused them with a pleasant aroma and flavor. We were satisfied and happy until we were all stricken with constipation a few days later. All of us had to huff and puff to have a bowel movement; many of us experienced rectal bleeding. The constipation further aggravated my already troubled rear end. All the blood in the latrine made it look like a fowl had just been slaughtered. Some of the more stubborn cases of constipation were relieved only with medical instruments. Surgery was done in two cases.

After the constipation crisis, plowing continued for about three months. Thousands of mu, mostly for rice paddies, were plowed. The drier land was for beans, corn, and other vegetables. A small area was allotted for a fruit orchard and a nursery. My brigade was located close to the dam. A little creek nearby was full of lovely bushes and wildflowers. But

November was extremely cold in this area; the creek froze over; the ground hardened. The field levelling work had to stop. All labourers turned to road-building and ditch-digging by excavating the frozen ground using a hammer to bore through the blocks. Production was measured by how many cubic meters of blocks you broke up.

HARSH WINTER

Our current job was to break up the frozen blocks for the irrigation ditches of the rice paddies. The work site was half an hour on foot from our shelters, so lunch was cooked and eaten in the field. The cooking facility was a hut in the middle of the field. The shattered door and windows were covered with rushes. The chilly air blew through the hut. The only light in the hut was from the burning hay for cooking. It was hard work for the prisoners assigned to this job, but they were better off than the rest of us, who had to work outside in the piercing cold.

Lunch consisted of salted congee made from corn powder and potato granules. This mixture was made specially to keep us warm. We could have three small bowls of congee, sufficient to fill us up. After everyone got his three bowls, the leftovers were offered to those still hungry. Thankfully, we were no longer using the ABC rationing scheme.

One night, a cold current moved in. We started work before dawn in the roaring wind. It was so cold that the only way we could find relief was by working harder. Because of the severe cold, local residents did not work for 27 days following the winter solstice, but we not only had to work but worked in the open air.

On that day, another squad member and I were on kitchen duty. At noon, we went to the cooking hut to get the food. The congee was in two kegs that were not too heavy, and which could be transported on a board. In order to distribute the congee, we had to remove our mittens to hold the bowl and ladle. The bowl had to be filled to the top and the congee pressed firm, to ensure that each bowl of congee was equal. If the portions were not equal, we might be accused of favoritism, and a quarrel might ensue. Our hands turned numb within minutes of removing our mittens.

By the afternoon, our hands still had not recovered; we could not even hold our hammers. For the rest of the day, we just did carrying work.

My "congee-serving" partner went back to the dorm 15 minutes earlier than the rest of us to prepare wash water for the group. He put his hands in a basin of hot water. His hands immediately turned from white to purple to black. Later, his hands festered with a bad odor. For a while, he was reassigned to a lighter job. During the reorganization in the spring, he was transferred to somewhere else, meaning that we would never see him again. He had been one of my closer working partners. The doctor told me his hands would have to be amputated.

According to the locals, frozen hands, feet, nose or ears should not touch hot water for a long time. The best way was to rub them with snow until they turned red. On that day, I came back with the rest of the group. In the camp, two small basins of water were provided for the 24 people in the squad. I objected strongly to this unhygienic way of using water, especially since one of the prisoners had a venereal disease. I never used the communal water and instead, used water from the ditch. Thus, on that cold day, I used melted snow instead of the warm basin water, which is why my hands were not destroyed.

Frostbite was a common occurrence in labor camps in that area. I had seen a number of prisoners with short fingers or toes, but they could still work. I had suffered some mild frostbite to my ears, painful and annoying at the time, but it did not result in permanent disfigurement. When I first came to this place, temperatures 30º C below zero (- 22º Fº) were common. Mercifully, in later years, the cold currents became less frequent.

THE GREAT LEAP FORWARD

Winter finally yielded to spring. It was time to prepare for sowing and planting. Our main task was to set up the small paddies of four mu each with embankments. Our brigade was responsible for ten thousand mu, about 700 mu per squad.1 This work assignment of thirty mu per capita

---

1 There are 0.0015 mu in 1 square meter; 1 mu is equal to 666.66666666667 square meter.

was the highest in the nation. In order to elevate our spirits, the office started feeding us better—potatoes, carrots, and cabbage stalks were added to our daily fare. The blight of marginal nutrition was over.

Around 1958, the government vigorously proclaimed the red banners of "Great Line for Socialist Construction," "the Great Leap Forward," and "the People's Commune." Among the three campaigns, the Great Leap Forward undoubtedly had the greatest impact on the reform-through-labor camps. This campaign was meant to inspire us to realize our potential by increasing production. The high commander ordered battalions to hold oath-taking rallies. For each squad, the initial phase was to write speeches and draft production quota guarantees. Squads and individuals were required to submit letters of determination. Challenge-and-acceptance campaigns were instituted between squads and between individuals. My squad spent a lot of time arriving at a quota guarantee. All favorable and adverse elements were carefully weighed. The final number was 800 catties (400 kilos). This impossibly high quota was never reached.

The rally field was well decorated. Red flags were blowing in the air. Slogans were posted all around. Because of the hot weather, the rally started in the evening. A battalion officer made the opening speech. He said that in order to accelerate the construction of a socialist society, Chairman Mao and the Central Committee of the Communist Party were calling upon the nation to sprint forward by hoisting the three red banners. We, the reform through labor prisoners could not be exempt. We must work hard to increase rice production. All the battalions, brigades, and squads were required to set up quotas to make a systematic effort to increase output.

What followed was that all the squads announced their commitment. The quotas given by the first few squads were around a thousand catties. Meanwhile, one of the officers interrupted to say that all must be brave enough to break free from the pillar of conservatism and aspire to loftier targets. From this insinuation, many began to raise their numbers. It was just like a frenzied auction house with ever-increasing bids. The numbers were increased five-fold. When the last offer of ten thousand catties came in, there was a burst of laughter. This wildly unrealistic quota was highly praised by the officers on the podium. The final act was the waging of challenge and acceptance campaigns. The speeches were reckless and incoherent. The meeting went on and on, finally breaking up shortly after midnight.

In the brigade meeting that was held shortly thereafter, it was proclaimed that those who made the initial commitments had been too conservative. They were exhorted to follow the example of the higher bidders. Later, the news reported that under the "Great Leap Forward," as advocated by Chairman Mao, an experimental rice farm in Tianjin had produced a record 200,000 catties per mu. Many were startled at this news. Instead, I only found it a mockery. At first, I had presumed that it was a fabrication of the reform administration. What baffled me was that the same story was publicized nationally in all the official papers. This absurd fantasy of 200,000 catties per *mu* was presented as an ironclad fact, a glorious achievement of Mao that would be handed down for generations.

"APPEAL" AND RE-SENTENCE

One day, the entire battalion was called into a meeting, our first meeting in quite some time. On a makeshift wooden platform, the officer announced through the loudspeaker, "The government, with its policy of allowing the full implementation of the judicial process, has decided to allow any of you who feel that his sentence was excessive or that the judicial process was unfair, to appeal within the next thirty days to the office that made the judgment. The battalion office will forward your appeals to the appropriate offices. But any unsubstantiated attempts to overturn a decision will result in additional punishment. Those who know how to write should write their own appeals; those who do not know may seek help from others with the office's approval. You have thirty days to apply."

When we were sentenced, we were told emphatically that no written judgment would be given and that no appeals would be allowed. The current reversal of that policy seemed strange. Questions swirled in my mind. As I recalled, when I was sentenced, even though no recorded judgment was given, there were only three charges in my case: 1) listening to the Voice of America and spreading rumours, 2) attempting to form a reactionary organization, and 3) planning to go to Hong Kong to join the insurgent forces.

At the beginning of the liberation, the government did not prohibit people from listening to foreign broadcasts. Nearly all my friends and colleagues with short-wave radios listened to the Voice of America. That was because the news they broadcast was truthful and detailed, and the broadcast signal was strong and clear. How could I be charged with something that the law did not prohibit? The charge of forming a reactionary organization had no substance whatsoever. As for my plan to join the insurgent force, it was true that I wanted to go to Hong Kong, but I had no intention of going to Taiwan. I also wanted to go to the U. S., but only so I could get a good job at the United Nations. At the height of the campaign to aid Korea and resist U. S. aggression, planning to go either to Taiwan or the U. S. was considered reactionary. It seemed to make little sense for me to make a defense based on that point. It looked like I had some grounds to launch an appeal—not for acquittal—but for a reduction of my sentence.

The next day after work many started to write. Most of those who decided to appeal had been charged with counterrevolutionary activities. Many of these prisoners had an insufficient educational background to write the appeals themselves. Why was the government reversing its policy and allowing us to appeal? Could it be to trap us? To decoy the snake out of its grotto was their old trick. Since the deadline for the appeal was nearly a month away, I decided to mull things over for a while.

While I was ruminating, I thought back to the previous treachery of the government. One case was the sudden closure of the Shanghai Stock Exchange. The Shanghai Stock Exchange was booming before the Communist takeover. After they came to power, many traders thought the stock exchange was incompatible with socialism and withdrew, causing stocks to fall rapidly. Nevertheless, the brokerage houses as well as the exchange kept their doors open despite the declining patronage. Unexpectedly, the government paid no attention to this activity, giving the impression of noninterference. Therefore, many of the traders went back into the market and the stock exchange again flourished. Without warning, one night the government sent a great number of soldiers and police to shut down the stock exchange and all the brokerage houses, confiscating all the stocks and securities, and all the gold and U. S. dollars. The government's treachery then made a big impression on me.

The other case of government deceitfulness that I recalled was the registration of reactionary groups. About a year after coming into power, the government called upon all the members of the Nationalist Party, the

Sanminzhuyi Youth Corp, and other organizations that were considered reactionary to register at their local police station. According to government propaganda, registration would remove the stigma of being a reactionary. But on April 27, 1951, before dawn—in the "great Search and Arrest—the government mobilized its armed forces and special service policemen throughout the country, sending them door to door, arresting everyone who had registered. When I was locked up at the Shanghai Police Station, I had met a Nationalist Party member who had been swept up in the "great search and arrest."

When I was with the Bureau of Taxation, I had witnessed its officers lying to the citizens. Telling the truth might stir up certain anxieties among the population that could cause operational difficulties. I had interjected my view that government should always tell its citizens the truth. At first, I was accused of lagging ideologically; later I was branded a reactionary; finally, I was labeled a counterrevolutionary, arrested, and imprisoned. Thus, my years of forced labor stemmed from my conviction that government should not deceive its citizens.

After prolonged reflection, I decided not to appeal my sentence. But with the office's approval, I wrote several petitions for other prisoners. Six months passed without a single word. After another few months, a meeting was called to announce the results. All the applicants waited breathlessly; there was dead silence. The officer announced the applicants who had received no change in their sentences, followed by those whose sentences had been increased. Not a single sentence was reduced. One person who had not appealed received an increased sentence because he had charged money to write appeals for others. The total number of cases was less than a hundred. The cases where judgments were stayed outnumbered those with added penalties. A number of appellants never received a report; they did not dare to make inquiries.

At the conclusion of the meeting, the commander said, "The number of people who took the opportunity to appeal was more than they had expected. Most of the appeals were without substance. The Party felt that groundless appeals were a deliberate attempt to stir up the evil wind of reversing correct decisions. This time, the Party was compassionate—most of the terms were kept at the original level. The added penalties were only a couple years. In the future, more severe punishment would be imposed upon similar cases." All appellants were deeply disappointed. Those who received the added penalties were demoralized, but they dared not show indignation.

Shortly thereafter, we had learning sessions attacking the opportunist appellants for trying to reverse correct decisions. During these sessions, I learned that a group of democrats in the higher echelon of government had advocated for allowing appeal of the sentences. But the Communists felt that questioning the original sentences was detrimental to a socialist country. This whole affair was reminiscent of Mao Zedong's "free expression" campaign.[2] Mao first encouraged people to freely air their views, and then he labeled them as rightists and swept them all out. The intellectuals were trusting and followed blindly, thus becoming clear targets for persecution.

From that point on, I became a respected figure among the cadres. They praised me for being an articulate intellectual with a high level of political consciousness who had not tried to appeal his sentence. It showed that I was cognizant of my own guilt, acting in line with my status as a reform laborer, and showing self-restraint. In later years, the supervisors implemented an annual merit system. That compliment of "cognizant of his own guilt, acting in line with his status as a reform laborer, and self-restraint" was on my record every year. But what tangible benefits I received from this compliment was hard to identify.

The rock-breaking job at Xishanzui was completed a few days before the Spring Festival. We had nothing to do except clean our living quarters in preparation for the festivities. At that time, the office informed us about a post-festival redeployment plan. People originating from the west would be sent to a farm in nearby Xishan (West Hill). Those from the east would be sent to the Baoanzhao farm in the northeast part of Inner Mongolia. The officer told us, 1) we were being switched from

---

2 The "free expression" campaign refers to the Hundred Flowers Campaign (百花运动, pinyin: bǎi huā yùn dòng) beginning in 1956. According to Mao, the Hundred Flowers Campaign was meant to promote the flourishing of the arts and the progress of science. For the first few months, the issues discussed in this campaign were minor and not of great importance. In the spring of 1957, Mao expressed that criticism of the government and its policy was preferred. All of a sudden, millions of letters began rolling in and the government was under fierce attack from students and intellectuals. Students at Peking University even dedicated a "Democracy Wall" in protest of Mao and the government. The Hundred Flowers Campaign abruptly ended in July 1957. Shortly thereafter, Mao launched the Anti-Rightist Campaign (反右派运动, pinyin: fǎn yòu pài yùn dòng). People who had been critical of the communist regime and ideology were labeled "rightists" and were persecuted.

construction work to farm work, 2) we would produce staple and auxiliary foods, meat as well as vegetables, and 3) we would have plenty to eat.

Our foremost concern was to have enough food. But how much truth was there in the officer's statement? Before we came to the west, we were told that there were plenty of cattle and sheep, but that we might be disappointed with the lack of vegetables. Then when we got here, there were no cattle or sheep. We could not rely on the rosy pictures the government painted of our future.

"VOLUNTARY" REQUEST TO REMAIN

The brigade I belonged to was at "Xing Shanties". Many years ago, it was the Xing's hometown. The head of the family bought many mu of land here and cultivated them. As part of this brigade, I cultivated rice for a several years. The work was difficult, but at least there were no uprisings or incidents. Most of the prisoners were assigned to transplant rice seedlings, while others worked in the nursery, vegetable garden, mess hall, clinic, in animal husbandry, or structural repair. Because I had no special skill, I remained in the rice paddies.

At 47º latitude, we were at the northernmost point in the world for rice paddies. Planting could not start until June. Harvesting was in mid-September. Many critical and intensive chores were done in between, such as removing mounds, weeding, irrigation, trenching, and insect control. Shelling was done in mid-November, when the temperature was already -10º C (+14 Fº). Before shelling could commence, water had to be poured over the field to create a sheet of ice. This prevented sand and soil from contaminating the grain. The shelling had to be done around the clock in order to complete it before mid-February; otherwise, the ice would melt and the rice would become soiled. Cultivating rice in that area was a race against time.

The burden of growing rice in an inhospitable climate was on our shoulders. During the planting month of June, the soil had not fully defrosted. Water in the field was close to the freezing point. Working barefoot in that water was injurious. Our feet were frozen red. Although I frequently had a cold, I was never granted sick leave. Shelling at night, when the temperature had dropped to -30º C (- 22º Fº), was pure agony. The ceaseless noise of the shelling mill thundered in my ears and jarred my mind. The hull, the awn, and the residual leaves and straw from the mill fogged the entire area. In the darkness and turmoil, work injuries were not uncommon, including severe injuries of arms mangled in the mill machinery.

The virgin soil, black and rich in humus, provided a high yield of about three hundred kilos per *mu* per year. But the prisoners were seldom entitled to the bounty of their labor. Because the quality of the rice was said to exceed the best rice from Wuxi, some was shipped to the Beijing market. A small portion was offered to the local officers and cadres. Only during important festivals and holidays, such as the Mid-Autumn festival, National Day, New Year, and Spring Festival, did the prisoners enjoy any of this excellent rice at one catty per person. Our diet of millet and corn was obtained locally by bartering our rice. We did not complain about eating only millet and corn. At least we were no longer being starved by the authorities, who increased the amount of our food because they were happy with the high rice yields.

Time went fast. We, the reform-through-labor prisoners, all had sentences of ten years or longer. Many of the prisoners convicted before 1950 were due for release. However, those whose terms were up, including me, were required to fill out a form called "Voluntary Request to Remain on the Farm for Continued Work."

After our "release," we moved from the enclave to the adobe houses immediately adjacent to the enclave. Our official status changed from prisoner to farmworker, but we did the same work as before. We were freed from the surveillance of armed guards, enjoyed a limited degree of movement, and received a monthly stipend of about ten yuan to take care of our provisions and clothing. Meals were taken at the dining hall of the farmworkers' camp. The food was a little better than what was offered to the prisoners but not by much.

Besides these differences, the type of work, the living schedule, the rules, and the study requirements were exactly the same as the prisoners'. Still wearing the label of "Four Undesirables," we remained under the restraint and instruction of the same brigade office. According to the rules, we were entitled to home leave, but in practice it was rarely granted. The rules stipulated that leave could not be granted to persons with any of these conditions: 1) less than five years since release from prison, 2) absence of immediate family, 3) unsatisfactory performance, and 4) inadequate adherence to the government.

What was really odious was that there were no tangible criteria for the last two conditions. It was up to the judgment of the cadres. Only a small percentage of the "ex-prisoners" were qualified to apply, and very few of those were ever approved. Even if all the restrictions had been waived, there were so many "ex-prisoners" that our turn for home leave would have come up once every twenty years.

When the prisoners due for release were required to "request to remain on the farm for continued work", those with wives and children declined to sign and pled with the cadres to be released outright, in order to be reunited with their families. Not only were the requests denied, but the pleaders were severely criticized.

One day, the battalion sent an officer to the brigade. He reported the following:

"Those who have fulfilled their imposed penalty must sign the application of 'Voluntary Request to Remain on the Farm for Continued Work' in order to continue your farm work. You are people with criminal records, the enemy of the people, and the dregs of society. No normal community can bear your presence as the Four Undesirables. Some of you were anxious to get back and declined to sign the required application. You insisted that the government grant your demand to return home. The government, with a powerful security force and an all-inclusive judicial network, would not submit to these threats. Would you fantasize about being thrown onto a big wave by eels? The government has repeatedly told you that you will have no place in any community, yet you still insist on going back. What are you really conspiring to do? Do you want to repeat the same thing you did, to commit another crime? This is clear evidence that you have not adequately reformed ideologically. We, the reformatory authority, are responsible for you and to society. We definitely cannot set you free after your evil deeds. It would endanger society, endanger the country. We are compelled to put you back into the reform process. It is solemnly declared that those whose terms are up must fill out the application to remain in the field for continued work. Otherwise, release will not be granted. You will have to undergo another round of ideological struggle to forgo your wishful thinking. When you have arrived at the right attitude and filled out the form, you will then be released."

After the meeting, one prisoner murmured, "It was a termed penalty; now it's a life sentence." Someone else said, "Since it's compulsory, what's the use of disguising it as voluntary?"

Soon after that, the few who had refused to sign surrendered. They came to realize that the government had all the power. If they continued to resist, things would get even worse for them. In the words of that cadre, they arrived at the right perception. For me to remain for continued work, after my sentence of 12 years was completed, was not a disaster because I did not have relatives or friends to return to. My parents had died in quick succession from the distress brought on by my imprisonment. I had no wife or children. I had a schizophrenic brother in Shanghai with a wife and daughter, but they were in such extreme poverty that they could not even take care of themselves. My niece was in primary school. My sister-in-law cleaned houses to support the family. I was one of the Four Undesirables and had no job. How could my brother possibly give me refuge? Because there was no place where I could go, I was at peace with being compelled to remain on the farm. But I did have a strong distaste for the government referring to the application as "voluntary."

I was arrested at the end of January, 1951. I was given a twelve-year sentence. After the new year of 1963, I was within days of my release. When I have something to look forward to, I find that time passes slowly. Besides, I worried that some miscarriage of justice might frustrate my partial liberation. Some prisoners had seen their release dates come and go for reasons such as 1) documents did not arrive on time, 2) disputes of release dates, or 3) misfiling of an added penalty.

It was the end of January 1963. I was experiencing both anxiety and elation. Normally, when a prisoner was due for release, notification would be sent from the office in the morning. The prisoner would then be excused from work, do his packing, go to the office to fill out the application for "Voluntary Request to Remain on the Farm for Continued Work," and get his "Certificate of Release". I did not receive the notice that morning, so I had to go to work with the rest of the squad. Extremely disappointed, I tried to figure out what was holding things up.

After lunch, I was called to the office, where the counselor told me, "You are due for release today. We sent a man to notify you this morning, but you had already left for the field. Go to the administration office to pick up your 'Certificate of Release' and then report to your new brigade."

I brought my belongings, along with three letters of introduction, to Wulan Farm, three kilometers away, to pick up my Certificate. Then I rushed to my assigned brigade. Here there was no enclosed wall, no police post, no electrified barbed wire, and no armed guards. It was not real freedom, but I could breathe a little easier. I was delighted to see some of my acquaintances who had been released earlier. From this point on, my reform process officially entered a new phase, the Second Reform through Labor – a new chapter in my life.

CHAPTER 8

FARMWORKER PERIOD

WORK POINTS

The work, education, and disciplinary measures were not much different at the Farmworkers Camp than at the reform-through-labor camps but my quality of life was improved somewhat. We all received a stipend of just over ten yuan per month. After buying food, there was a little money left to buy clothing and other necessities. Some of my fellow workers used the money to smoke and drink while their clothes fell apart. The little bit of freedom made me feel better.

But, as usual, the good days did not last long. Under the Rules of the People's Commune, the system of fixed output and division of labor were implemented. Fixed wages were eliminated. Our annual compensation was based on the production credits we earned. Our base salary covered only the cost of food. I would not know the amount of my bonus until the end of the year. The production credit system was an obtuse monster. Each squad was allotted ten points multiplied by the number of workers in the squad. For example, if a squad had twenty people, the squad was allotted 200 points. Then we had to decide how to allocate the points among each other based on productivity.

Every evening, we appraised our productivity, taking time from our learning sessions. Not surprisingly, squabbles broke out during every appraisal session, sometimes escalating into fistfights. Often, we would argue deep into the night. Dejected and sleep-deprived, we became less productive in our farm work. During the days of food rationing, I had hoped for a good meal; now I was longing for a good night's sleep. During the appraisals, I always kept silent. When my points were rated, I raised my hand to show my accord with the group's assessment. These late nights dragged on until the end of year.

After the Spring Festival, the brigade statistician, along with the point recorders of each squad, calculated the annual remuneration for every individual. The amount, after deducting the cost of food, ranged from 20 to 40 yuan per person. I received just under 30 yuan. We had all been hoping for a bonus of around 100 yuan for the year.

The accounting, which was made public, showed that production costs ate up the lion's share of the income, leaving only a meagre amount for our bonuses. We had no way of verifying the accounting but were afraid to question it; after all, we were one of the "Four Undesirables."[1]

The appraisal system continued into a second year, but we had appraisal meetings only once a week—on Saturday evening. This was definitely a better arrangement, as we were able to sleep well the other nights of the week, which resulted in our being more productive. Since we knew the yearly bonus would be a miserly amount, we didn't bother squabbling over the appraisals.

In the fall, for unknown reasons, the appraisal system was eliminated and wages were reinstated. This change was reported to have been initiated by Liu Shaoqi, who was criticized by the officials for doing so. The new wage system worked as follows: The starting pay was 25 yuan per month and the next level was 31. Those with extra merit were paid 35. Those who were inefficient received 22. At first, I was paid 31 but later was downgraded to 25 for unknown reasons. Everyone received more under this system; furthermore, we were free of appraisals and the discord that came with them.

The year 1966 saw the advent of the Cultural Revolution.

It was an ideological purification campaign created and conducted personally by Chairman Mao. Mao was a political genius, inventing one novel political campaign after another. The Cultural Revolution was unprecedented, both in scale and duration. Even though the labor prisons and farm camps were in obscure places, isolated from the rest of the country, some of the things that happened in these quarters were ridiculous as well as terrifying.

---

[1] In 1958, the Chinese government designed a campaign to rid the "four undesirables", namely mosquitoes, flies, rats, and sparrows. The official propaganda claimed that China's quest for rapid industrialization during the Great Leap Forward must not be hindered by the "four undesirables", believed to be affecting crop production. Here, the author used the "four undesirables" as rhetoric to indicate his unwelcome status during the Great Leap Forward.

FOUR CLARIFICATION CAMPAIGN

After the "Great Leap Forward, our life was peaceful for a while. On the eve of the new year, we had a big snowstorm that lasted for two days and nights. The snow was knee-deep. What followed was a severe cold wave. The doors and windows of our adobe huts shattered. Roofs were blown away. The temperature outside dropped to -30º C (- 22º Fº). We were told there would be no work. Everyone was ecstatic. The blizzard was so severe that the cadres and guards were not willing to be out on the field.

Instead, next day after lunch, a meeting was called to make a "mobilization report of winter reprimand," dealing specifically with the "Four Clarification Campaign." We learned at the meeting that the "four clarifications" referred to clearing up matters that were political, organizational, economic, and ideological. Ironically, these topics were not really relevant to the prisoners but only to party members, cadres, and government employees. Because through repeated trials and investigations, constant surveillance, and the unreserved confessions and merciless disclosures, the problems of the prisoners had long been crystal clear.

The camp administration took the "Four Clarification Campaign" very seriously. Slogans were posted everywhere. Campaign cries were shouted, such as "do it in a big way" and "enforce it in a sweeping manner." One cadre per squad oversaw the proceedings. The way to "clarify" was to have each prisoner make self-criticism on each of the four categories. Other members of the squad might "counsel" the criticism so that the person was denounced further. The written material and responses were compiled for official approval. The insignificant and less involved prisoners came first, followed by the complicated cases. Those whose self-criticism was approved were commended as being "liberated." Those whose self-criticism was deemed unacceptable were required to engage in further self-criticism and ideological struggle before being approved.

During the campaign, lights in the dorms were on throughout the night. Armed guards kept watch, as the authorities feared that some of us would attempt suicide or escape. I could not fall asleep with the lights on and suffered unrelenting fatigue and dizziness during the day.

The cadres waged psychological warfare by saying that those who did not open-heartedly confess would divulge their crimes at night while delirious or dreaming. In this round of investigation the authorities wanted to uncover any previously unknown reactionary activities of the prisoners. But even if we had not concealed any inappropriate words or deeds, we were nevertheless coerced, attacked, and insulted. I had no hidden misdeeds, but I still had to go through this "clarification" agony. I was one of the first to be called to the office for the "clarification" proceedings. I passed the criticism and struggle session in just a day and a half.

The cadre supervising my session told me, "You are now liberated. Counsel others without reservation during the inquisition of their cases. Make your criticism strict and rigorous. If you work as instructed, it will imbue the proceedings with great momentum. Let there not be any stagnant moments. Carry this campaign thoroughly and in depth. You have been approved. Nobody can counterattack."

I was greatly relieved by this smooth passage but revolted that he wanted me to make unwarranted attacks on others. I had many times been a victim of such treachery; how could I use it now against others? Since there was no official rule saying that I must follow this instruction, I took a wait-and-see approach. To place a villain into a group to intensify the struggle was an established scheme of the Communists. More often than not, the assignee made loud accusations against the targeted parties, and sometimes this escalated into an assault. I did not use this opportunity to get even, display socialist enthusiasm, or win favor with the supervisors. Sometimes, the struggle on a single case might last several days and nights. Many failed the clarification process.

Clarification continued for one and a half months. The lunar New Year was approaching. The winter reprimands came to an end and heavy labor resumed. The camp administration proclaimed that the clarification work would resume later with even more vigor. The only reason for the hiatus was so that there would be more time for heavy labor; no pending cases were ever reopened. To my knowledge, no injury or death occurred during this campaign, in contradistinction to the many injuries and deaths that resulted from the "Suppression of Counterrevolutionaries," "Purge of Counter-revolutionaries," "Combat Deviations to the Right," and, later, the Cultural Revolution.

THE THREE ALLEGIANCES

At the beginning of the Cultural Revolution, I was in the *Datu Bao* (Big Adobe Fort) brigade of *Baitu Gang* (White Earth Hill). The cadres, in order to expound on the significance and importance of the Cultural Revolution, called frequent meetings of the entire battalion and gave instructions to the brigades. Each squad was then required to discuss what they had learned.

We had to study Chairman Mao' writings and quotations. Each of us received a copy of Quotations from Chairman Mao, also known as the Precious Red Book. The "Old Three Essays"—"A Foolish Man Determined to Move the Mountain', 'Be at the Service of the People', and 'Remember Dr. Bethune'—were especially extolled and had to be memorized. Mistakes were not tolerated. At the evening study sessions, we had to hold the book and sit up straight; leaning against the wall was forbidden.

During these sessions, everyone was required to state his position, make self-criticism, and receive criticism from others. After we were utterly exhausted, the study period was extended another two or three hours to "break our backs." From my experience throughout the years, I came to understand that the ruling echelon was always worried that peace might endow us common people. They racked their brains out to make sure that this did not happen. They wanted to afflict pain and mistreat people, and sometimes even put them to death. What led to this type of behaviors is hard to comprehend. Could it just be that they were sadistic?

Before long, there was a new ritual. Every morning before washing up, we had to bow three times in front of Mao's portrait, recite a few of his quotations, and sing revolutionary songs. This concluded with our chanting "Long Live Chairman Mao." Before going to bed, a similar ritual was repeated in assembly. These became a part of our daily life for years. It did not stop until the end of the Cultural Revolution when the Lin Biao incident occurred. When something strange is repeated many times, it became a part of our lives, and the bizarreness faded.

What followed was the Three Allegiances Campaign. They were 1) boundless allegiance to Chairman Mao, 2) boundless allegiance to the thoughts of Chairman Mao, and 3) boundless allegiance to the

Communist Party. Workers were required to develop ingenious ways to demonstrate their loyalty, such as through writing, painting, poetry, songs, paper cutting, etc. An "Allegiance Dance" was developed. The "Song of Allegiance" was even more popular.

Because of my good calligraphy, I was assigned to write banners in color with the pleasing slogans of "the Great Leader, the Great Tutor, the Great Commander, the Great Helmsman（伟大的领袖、伟大的导师、伟大的统帅、伟大的舵手）" I had to be extremely careful when I wrote these titles, as any mistake could induce severe punishment. One absent-minded writer misspelled the character "great"（大）. In Chinese, the character "great"（大）and the character "dog"（犬）differs by only one dot. The person who wrote the character "dog"（犬）instead of "great"（大）was accused of "attacking" the Communist Party. The Chinese character "nation"（国）consists of three symbols that represent "territory," "people," and "defense forces." During the Japanese invasion, the Japanese introduced a new character, replacing this symbol with a sign of "king"（王）. Since "king" was not compatible with socialism, the Communists added a dot to the symbol "king"（王）and changed it into the symbol "jade"（玉）. A writer who missed that dot was accused of fantasizing the return of the feudalistic monarch system.

One time, the character Mao（毛）, the last name of our Chairman, has a hook-like stroke in the lower right. Once, a paper-cut on the wall had its lower right side dangling. The maker was accused of wishing that Chairman Mao would become a cripple and the Communist would Party fall. This was one of many examples. Such people were severely criticized, and the incidents were written up and filed as evidence of counterrevolutionary tendencies.

One sunny Sunday, the workers were using their precious day off (alternate Sundays) to wash dirty clothes, which were hung on trees, sticks, or suspended cords. Another man and I carelessly hung our laundry on the board of Mao quotations. This was considered an act of flagrant contempt, and we were reported to the office. That evening, we were vociferously condemned and vigorously beaten. The other fellow had hung his underwear and socks, while I had merely hung my cap, so I was punished less severely. But both of us had this incident put in our files.

One day, the brigade was assembled to hear a report. In addition to the regular officers, a soldier in his twenties from the Liberation Army was present. An officer introduced him as the pacesetter for learning the writings of Chairman Mao. He had been invited to instruct us in the writings of Chairman Mao. The soldier, who might have been a student, was gentle and serene. He was a bit bashful in the beginning but quickly gained his composure. His talk was full of platitudes but nothing inappropriate or objectionable. The only detectable flaw might be that his talk was a little too plain. After he left, the officer spoke highly of him and said that he has many engagements for this talk every day and that he could recite the "Old Three Essays" fluently since he knew the material "inside out." He knew how many paragraphs and how many words there were in each essay, and even knew the exact number of "de" (的), which is used as a possessive and in several other contexts. The counselor praised the soldier's extensive knowledge, and challenged us to follow suit. Thereafter, a wave of learning the "Old Three Essays" ensued. We were required to memorize them. After two weeks, this excitement over the "Essays" dissipated.

After learning the Three Allegiances and the writings of the Chairman, we entered the phase of exposure and criticism, which should have been called "the period of terror."

DENUNCIATION CAMPAIGN

This period was inaugurated by a mobilization meeting, during which the officers detailed the procedures and methods of exposure and criticism. During the process, all culprits would be sternly criticized. All cases of wrongdoing would be thoroughly investigated. No innocent party would be falsely implicated, but the wicked would not go unpunished. The officers quoted Mao, "Revolution is not a dinner party, not essay writing, not picture painting, and not embroidery. It cannot be that graceful, that easy, that leisurely, and that civilized. It cannot be temperate, kind, courteous, restrained, and magnanimous. Revolution is a riot—a class struggle of one class to overturn the other."

At that meeting and during subsequent instructions, the cadres hinted at the violent nature of the exposure-criticism sessions. Participants were told that gentleness was ineffectual and that reasoning alone was insufficient. Coercive forces must be added. During this process, procedures and methods had to be continuously intensified. Those being criticized were not allowed to stand up straight. Their heads had to remain bowed, and they were sometimes forced to kneel as a show of apology. At a later stage, humiliation was elevated to a level that included "flying an airplane" and wearing mud necklaces. If the culprit did not adequately defend himself during the inquisition, he was battered, kicked, and even flogged. The torture intensified at each and every stage. Monitors for labor, monitors for learning, and the activists who clung to the government controlled the meetings. In addition to inflicting high-handed abuse, they also instigated others to escalate their atrocities. Those who were lukewarm about this were criticized for being kind-hearted and sympathetic toward those who had fallen behind ideologically. Reports of kind-heartedness were filed as another case for future sessions. For that reason, everyone had to shout and pretend to be one of the furious attackers.

At one of these struggles, I fell asleep on the sofa and began to snore. I was yanked off the sofa and beaten. Luckily, the next day was a rest day, so when the meeting resumed on Monday, everyone had forgotten about my "crime" of falling asleep on the sofa.

There was a good-hearted man in my squad named Mr. Zhang, with whom I had a good rapport. At one of the meetings, he was physically attacked and severely injured. When the bell for adjournment was about to ring I said, "Let's stop. We'll continue tomorrow evening." These words angered the attacker. He came over to hit me. I fought back in self-defense. The bystanders, without going to his support, intervened to calm us down to keep the fight from escalating. The next day, the attacker reported the incident, accusing me of sympathizing with those who had fallen behind ideologically. I was reprimanded. The education monitor confided to me that because of this, I was put on the black list for criticism and repudiation.

In general, those being attacked were gentle and virtuous. The cruel and malignant ones were spared because the rest were afraid of retaliation. During the exposure-criticism period, fear and horror were ever-present. Fortunately, no tragedies took place in my squad. Physically torturing our comrades and stripping them of their dignity was widespread. Nobody brought up the archaic idea of due process or human rights.

Someone in the squad next to us was accused of some crime. He obstinately refused to admit his guilt, thus prolonging the meetings for 1½ months. His nightly beatings left him with a swollen face and a limp. He looked stupefied. Two guards stayed with him day and night to prevent escape, assassination, or suicide. During the struggle meetings, I could hear him screaming as he was beaten and tortured. He was a straightforward, guileless person and I had a fairly good relationship with him. His misfortune pierced my heart like a dagger. Of course, I was powerless to help him.

Two accused men from another squad were put into cells for not admitting their guilt. The cells were built at the beginning of the Cultural Revolution specifically for this purpose. Each cell was a four-square meter brick enclosure with no window, light, or electricity. The two men were frequently taken out to be harassed. Their case was complicated and involved many associates. I dared not ask for the details. A few days later, when a mess hall worker brought breakfast, he found one person comatose and the other had hung himself. An investigation revealed that the two had torn their shirts into strips, with which they hung themselves. One did not die because the strips tore. It was assumed that they were willing to die so that they would not be forced to disclose their accomplices. Such cases were branded by the authorities as "suicides afraid of punishment."

In another case, some workers, in handcuffs and shackles, were taken away by armed guards in a truck. Their squad did not know the reason they were removed. We never heard about them afterward. All these events terrified me and my fellow "voluntary" farmworkers. Whenever we heard a siren, we feared that we would be taken away. A family member of a farmworker, a lady in her 50s, screamed in terror every time she heard the siren. Her high-pitch cry was sickening to hear. After numerous such episodes, she went insane.

At that time, the Communists spared no effort in instituting a new system of investigation called "examining within and probing without." Investigators thoroughly investigated the most insignificant cases. My social contacts were quite limited. But still, some investigators came from Shanghai to question me. I did not even know some of the people they asked me about; I had no information to divulge. The people who came to make inquiries accused me of being dishonest, sly, and disloyal to the government—of protecting the guilty even after years of reformation.

One time someone from Shanghai came to ask me about an old

friend, Mr. Chao. My written report was rejected several times for being too scanty. Finally, I told them that this was all I knew and that I would not fabricate something to falsely implicate Mr. Chao. The investigator later complained to the office. As it turned out, Mr. Chao had joined the Communist Party in the early days when it was fighting the Japanese. Since the higher-ups of the Party suspected its members in respectable positions, how could they ever trust anyone outside the Party?

During the Cultural Revolution, the competition between party members and cadres was fierce. People with ambition took advantage of the chaos and pushed others out for their own advancement. Others saw it as a good chance to be admitted to the Party. There was an officer Fang in the main office who was not a party member. He looked vicious and was treacherous. At the beginning of the Cultural Revolution, he positioned himself as a leader of the revolutionary faction and touted himself as a leftist. He ran here and there in the name of conducting investigations while treating the farmworkers cruelly. He assaulted, cursed, and slapped them. Everyone was afraid of him. Even other cadres conceded to him. He attacked a cadre in a higher position, aspiring to replace him after he was expelled. This type of grappling for power was common throughout the Cultural Revolution.

During a struggle, a Mr. Qian at the office of the third brigade had pieces of his scalp pulled off. After that, he always wore a hat, even on the hottest days. I teased that he was lucky to be married, as his appearance would scare away all prospects.

At first, this "exposure and criticism" program was aimed at every person in the brigade. When about one-third of the group was done, the authorities changed to a more selective approach. They realized that if everybody had to go through the process, it could only be done perfunctorily. They wanted the criticism and repudiation to be deep and thorough in order to attain the desired deterrent effect. Those selected for censuring would undergo severe scrutiny and punishment. Every case had to be escalated to the anti-Party and anti-government level. So the criticism and repudiation of one person often took two weeks. For more complicated cases or when there was strong resistance, the process took even longer. An education monitor of another squad, with whom I had maintained good relations, told me that my name was on the list. Luckily, before my turn came up, I was transferred from *Datubao* to the third brigade of the Wulan Farm.

COMMISSAR WANG

After I was transferred to the third brigade of the second detachment of Wulan Farm, its Commissar, a man in his 60s named Wang, was accused of being a capitalist. He was isolated, interrogated, and forced to endure repeated criticism, repudiation, assaults, and curses. He became haggard and reduced to a skeleton. I had worked with him briefly when we attempted to develop an apparatus to transplant seedlings. I knew him to be a fine and principled gentleman.

In the winter of that year, he made his escape. His successful escape under close surveillance surprised everyone. Two guards were with him day and night, even when he used the toilet, but it was from there that he made his escape.

The latrine of the brigade was built against a wall of the compound. Excrement ran from the hole to a pit outside the wall. The cleanup work was done outside the latrine. In the winter, the waste matter froze up instantly. Mr. Wang slipped himself out through the hole one night while the two guards waited outside the latrine. When he did not come out of the latrine, the guards went in with a flashlight. He was gone. Since there was no other egress, they knew that he had crept out through the latrine hole. To pursue him, they would have to go through that hole or go through the front gate, which was a long distance from that spot. Since considerable time had already passed, the chance of catching him in the dark was small, so they did not pursue him.

If he had not made this courageous move, he would have been sentenced to death. His escape was carefully thought out. He waited until the weather was cold and the stool pit was frozen before taking the plunge. Afterward, he went to Beijing and hid in a friend's house. Shortly thereafter, the Lin Biao incident occurred, the Cultural Revolution ended, Mao died, and the Gang of Four fell; Mr. Wang was able to return to his original post.

After his escape, his wife, who was in her 40's, became the target of a struggle. She was a good-natured doctor and pharmacist, who was never contemptuous toward the farmworkers. Before the Communists came to power, she had been a high senior official. She owned an imitation camel hair coat and a pair of not-so-high heel shoes that were popular with young ladies before the Communists. Once, when I went out, I saw many people gathered in the square. Posters were all over and loudspeakers were blaring; it was clearly another public criticism session. On closer look, I saw that she was the target. No woman had been so brutalized before; the scene startled me. They cursed her as the witch of the bourgeoisie, threw her coat and her shoes on the ground, and ordered her to put them on and do a *Yangge* dance.[2] Although a gentle person, she would not submit to this coercion; she refused to dress up and dance. The revolutionaries forcefully put the shoes and coat on her. She kicked away the shoes and threw down the coat. They pressed her to the ground and rolled her all around and dragged her by her legs. She was covered all over with dirt and blood. The torture did not stop until she was almost on her last gasp. A few of the cadres in the office condemned this inhumane treatment, but nobody dared to intervene.

THE CULTURAL REVOLUTION'S AFTERMATH

One night, at a special meeting, the officer declared that anyone who still had pamphlets of Vice-Chairman Lin Biao's quotations should turn them in. Everyone was puzzled. Lin was second only to Mao. His quotations were almost as important as Mao's. I immediately sensed that Lin must be in some political turmoil. But I never would have dreamt that he had plotted to kill Mao, fled abroad, and died en route after the conspiracy was discovered. Thereafter, the exposure-criticism struggles and Three Allegiances Campaigns subsided. The purge of the leftists also abated.

During this period of great turmoil, I was incredibly fortunate to be spared any serious attacks, considering my family background, personality, education, work experience, sympathy for those accused, apathy toward reform, and insufficient affinity for the government.

The Cultural Revolution was a grandiose act of political persecution that came from political infighting inside the higher levels of the

---

2 Yangge (Chinese: 秧歌; pinyin: Yānggē) is a form of Chinese folk dance popular in northern China.

Communist Party. It brought untold suffering to ordinary citizens. Within my limited social contacts, I knew three people who killed themselves as a direct result of Mao's Cultural Revolution.

The first was the wife of my friend. Because of her husband's reactionary past, she was secluded and interrogated to reveal her husband's guilty deeds. A debilitated lady with frail nerves, she could not bear the torment. She jumped out of the third-floor window of her home, falling onto a concrete slab, smashing her skull, and dying instantly. The second suicide was the wife of my cousin, who also killed herself by jumping out of a window. The third was my brother's neighbor, who also jumped to his death. The sheer number of lives ruined by the Cultural Revolution was staggering.

My being alive with my sanity intact, after undergoing thirty years of oppression, is no less than a miracle. An old Chinese proverb says, "Late-in-life prosperity will be endowed upon those who do survive great calamity." It was now mid-1970. I was sixty years old. I had become frail and shaky, truly unfit to continue farm labor. But retirement was not an option; we were mandated to work until death. The authorities were unable or unwilling to find a light job on the farm for me. I was frequently criticized for my slow, inefficient performance. I told myself to persevere with the painfully arduous tasks, but this kind of life could not go on much longer.

CHAPTER 9

APPEAL AND EXONERATION

END OF THE CULTURAL REVOLUTION

In the fall of 1976, the office announced that Chairman Mao was dead. All these years, people were accustomed to shouting, "Long live, long live, long live Chairman Mao." There were no reports of his illness. Many people had the impression that he was not only healthy but almost immortal. They could not believe that he was dead. They saw the announcement of his "death" as a trick, once again, to detect their hidden feelings. On the other hand, the farm laborers saw the news as a gift from heaven, but no one dared to reveal his joy. We did not even discuss his death; everyone remained mute, lest any inadvertent expression incurred horrible consequences. I was secretly ecstatic, foreseeing a thorough transformation for the better sweeping through China now that Mao was dead. Mao's rule had culminated in the Cultural Revolution, a human tragedy of unparalleled scale.

Mao, an ardent student of history, knew well of China's feudalistic past. His adoption of Tiananmen Square as the icon of the nation was a glaring revelation of his infatuation with the pomp and majesty of a monarch. I did not consider Mao an intellectual; intellectuals perceive democracy, rule-by-law, and human rights as essential to the tranquility of a modern society.

Soon after Mao's death, the Gang of Four fell, followed by the conclusion of the Cultural Revolution. The Four Undesirables were eliminated and civilian rights were restored. There was reason for exhilaration and hope. The government and the courts called on people who had been falsely implicated and unjustly imprisoned to file appeals for exoneration. The new group in power wanted to heal a torn society, a step unimaginable under Mao. Many of those who appealed were exonerated. But I was ambivalent about an appeal. For decades, the feuds within the Communist ruling circle often led to the opposite side being branded as counterrevolutionary. If I appealed and lost, my name would be further blackened. While under the reform through labor campaign, I had set this precept for myself: "Rather be in prison than be submissive." I gave up the idea of appealing.

APPEAL

A few months later a meeting was held on the farm to celebrate the "Exoneration of the Wrongly Branded Four Undesirables." After that, I was granted a leave. It enabled me to go to Beijing, Shanghai, and Suzhou to visit my friends and relatives. All of them urged me to file an appeal. I then realized that my record reflected badly upon my social circle, so I began to draft a brief.

On this trip, I learned in greater detail what happened to my family after my arrest. Their outcome was typical of the misery endured by many of the oppressed intellectuals after the so-called Liberation. I had an older brother, who was married. While I was in prison, they had a daughter, an only child. My mother and father were alive when I went to prison. By the time I visited my hometown after my discharge, my family had all died except for my niece, who had married. From my niece, friends, and neighbors, I got a rough idea of what had happened to my family.

After my arrest, the office where I worked, the Shanghai Bureau of Direct Taxation, exhaustively searched my living quarters for evidence of my being a spy. Then a squad was sent to my hometown to look for evidence of counterrevolutionary activities, such as arms, communications equipment, and propaganda material. They found none. The squad interrogated my family, who had nothing to tell about my alleged involvement. My mother never recovered from the trauma of the interrogation; the shock left her depressed and anorexic. She died two years later from heart disease.

My father had worked for the Nationalist Government. After the Communist takeover, he worked as a tutor for a family. After my conviction, he was classified as the relative of a criminal and therefore lost his job. One time, when he was with a few friends in a teahouse, he said angrily, "I am his father. I know him. He is definitely not an agent. The charge is false." He accused the government of being undemocratic and not respecting human rights. Soon after, the police locked him up. Someone must have reported him. He died in jail. My niece found out from her mother that when my father was buried, his thin clothing was stained with blood. It looked as if he was beaten to death by the wardens.

During the Nationalist regime, my brother taught English at Fudan University, and worked at the American Embassy and United Nations Relief and Rehabilitation Administration (UNRRA) in Nanking. After the Communist liberation, he joined the Trade Department of China's eastern region. He was accused of idolizing foreigners and being a lackey of American imperialists. My counterrevolutionary status stained him further, resulting in more discrimination and insults. With each degradation and salary decrease, his mental health deteriorated, culminating in schizophrenia. During the Cultural Revolution, he was labeled a "counterrevolutionary". He was told that his crimes caused his mental illness. These accusations further traumatized him. He received a very small stipend, far from enough to support his wife, daughter, and mother-in-law. To supplement their income, my sister-in-law did housework for a neighbor. Not long after, her mother died due to lack of medical care. Then my sister-in-law was found to have ovarian cancer. My niece took her all over for treatment but was turned away because she was from a family of "counterrevolutionaries". Her cancer metastasized enlarging her stomach as if she were pregnant. When she died my niece was still young. She and my brother often did not have enough to eat. During the "Red Terror", she had just finished junior high school. In order to lighten the family burden, she went with a production team to the countryside. My brother lost his housing because he couldn't pay the rent and had to move to a 10 square meter dilapidated room with a mud floor. He lived from meal to meal. With some luck, upon her return, my niece joined a printing factory. Soon after, my brother died from longstanding malnutrition. My niece was left alone to fend for herself.

For my appeal, I needed a copy of the original judgment. Since I had never received the written judgment, I was obliged to ask the brigade office for a copy of the document. When I received it, I was dismayed to find out that it was quite different from the version read to me at sentencing. The version at sentencing was short and simple, while the filed one was greatly exaggerated, containing many fabrications. I could no longer write the appeal as planned. I had to write it by responding point by point to the written judgment. Because it contained false allegations, I

Chapter 9 *Appeal and Exoneration*

had great difficulty coming up with an objective and clear appeal. About a month after it was mailed, I received a reply saying that the appeal was filed and under review and that I should patiently await the court's decision. Nearly a year later, I received a notice asking me to appear in court.

EXONERATION

Filled with hope and excitement, I rushed to Shanghai and went with my niece to meet the clerk of the court. He told me that after review, the case was settled. He gave me a hearing date and asked me to be there. On the day of the hearing, I again went with my niece to court. The hearing was held in a small chamber. The clerk read the court's decision:

"1. The Reviewed Criminal Case Decision of the Higher People's Court of Shanghai: So-and-so was sentenced by the Commander of the Liberation Army of Shanghai District on dd, mm, yy, with the decision of a twelve-year term of servitude for his counterrevolutionary design. The convicted has filed an appeal in this court. After review, we found the original judgment invoked an inappropriate law, and we, therefore, decided to revoke the judgment made by the Commander of the Liberation Army of the Shanghai District, and to return the case to the Shanghai District Court for review.

2. Reviewed Decision of Shanghai District Criminal Court:

"Because of the inappropriate law invoked, the Higher People's Court revoked the original judgment and returned the case to this court for review on dd, mm, yy. After due consideration, we found that so-and-so did make inappropriate statements but with no ill design of a counterrevolutionary nature. It was purely an educational and ideological problem. We, therefore, declare so-and-so acquitted."

After the acquittal pronouncement, I was given copies of the judgments. Suddenly, I saw a group picture on the officer's table. The picture was from my file. Startled to see such a picture in my file, I picked it up and studied it. The officer teased me, "See whether you are in it." His question made me a little anxious. I was sure that I was never in a group picture like that. I told him, "I never had a picture taken of me with that group. How could this be in my file? It must be a fabrication." At that point, he snatched the picture from me and put it back in the packet, saying "We knew you were not in it. If you were, the case would be much more serious." I asked again, "Could you let me see the picture? I didn't see what the caption said." He replied, "You have been acquitted. What do you want to see it for?" Then he walked out of the room.

Photographic forgery was not a very difficult trick, even in those days. If it were, how could they take Chairman Mao across the Yangtze so easily? The original judgment read at the time of pronouncement was very short, even shorter than at the time of my first sentence. At the end of the session, I asked the officer how the judgment could be so short. He told me that it was the first one. So, in total, there were four different judgments on my case. The first was the one the officer read to me at this acquittal. The second was the one read on my first sentencing at the prison. The third was the one on re-sentencing a few days later. The last was the one filed with the third brigade office. Each time, the judgment got more elaborate than the one before. It was grotesque and unjust.

After being exonerated, I left the farm and went to work as an English teacher in a school set up by the Bureau of Reform through Labor. Leaving the second reform through labor behind, I returned to society after thirty years of captivity.

AFTERWORD

Not long after I had begun writing this book, spring weather arrived. Since it was a good time to take a break, I went on a trip with my family and friends. On our way back, we stayed at the foothills of Yellow Mountain (黄山). While having dinner at a restaurant, we overheard a group of young people saying that college students in Beijing had gone on strike – demonstrating, and demanding that the Chinese government make democratic reforms, punish corrupt officials, enforce the laws, and protect human rights. The scale of the protest and the number of participants were unprecedented. Since our group had been traveling and touring places of interest, we hadn't read the newspapers, listened to the radio, or watched TV. We had been completely out of touch with domestic and international affairs for many days. Now we suddenly heard this startling news. My group and I became extremely excited. Ordinarily, when we talk about politics and domestic affairs, we grumble, complain, and get discouraged. Intellectuals, especially elite college students, are known to be passionate, knowledgeable, and insightful about politics – and to abhor dictatorship. They are unconcerned about winning or losing, unafraid of persecution, willing to take risks: they speak the truth. We were moved by their bravery and admired their boldness to openly express the grievances and aspirations we've all had for decades.

After I returned to Beijing, I took an early bus to Gongzhufen Station and planned to take the eastbound bus to Tiananmen Square to see the situation with my own eyes. Unexpectedly, no eastbound traffic could pass through Tiananmen Square. We had to take the subway instead. The subway station was extremely crowded with long lines at the ticket booths. We had to squeeze into the train, which did not stop at the next three stations; then finally stopped at Chongwen Station. I hurriedly squeezed my way out of the train and station, crossed East Chang'an Boulevard, turned at Taijichang Street, and headed west. Before reaching Tiananmen Square, a few dozen yards from the west end of Dongjiaomin Lane, I saw tens of thousands of people moving. I felt overwhelmed by the massive sea of humanity. When I entered the square, I saw waves of people, never before having seen anything on such a spectacular scale. Countless groups of people from schools, factories, and businesses filled the square. I saw a staggering number of flags and banners and heard singing, speeches, and slogans booming from countless loudspeakers. On the other hand, there was complete order, devoid of chaos. In the middle of the square were countless tents of various sizes, filled with out-of-town students or group members. They surrounded the Monument to the People's Heroes. I walked through the crowd and crossed to the other side. Large-character posters and small-character ones were plastered on the entrances, exits, and walls. All the slogans, speeches, large- and small-character posters demanded pro-democracy reforms, human rights protection, rule of law, free speech, free press, and the routing out of corrupt officials: these all aligned with the people's aspirations. So it is no wonder that the protest had won universal support. Thousands of people on the side of the road were clapping to express their support. I had left home at 7 a.m. Now five hours later, I was squeezed into a stream of people and followed them westward for an hour to finally arrive at Liubu Gate.

Processions and motorcades were pouring into the square. They held high-flying flags and placards. and chanted slogans. The atmosphere was jubilant. I was elated. After years of holding in grievances, indignation, and dissatisfaction, not daring to say what I wanted to say, now workers, teachers, intellectuals of all kinds, and the masses were openly, recklessly, whole-heartedly shouting and expressing their thoughts. It was heartwarming, exciting, and inspiring.

I had no way of estimating the number of people. But to fill the vast Tiananmen Square and the wide East and West Chang'an Road, there had to be at least several hundreds of thousands. That night radio stations reported that more than one million people were there. To witness this event was the most meaningful and memorable experience of my life. When I got home that evening, I was exhausted but happy.

In the next few days, because of my family's dissuasion, I did not go back to Tiananmen Square, instead only read large-character posters on the streets and listened to the news at the nearby Renmin University. Even these places had massive crowds. At one of these moments, news came that because the government was ignoring the various demands, twenty or thirty students were now on a hunger strike, and the number was growing. As soon as I heard this, I anticipated that the situation would soon change drastically.

This time, I took the subway from Xizhi Station to Chongwen Station and it went smoothly. As soon as I entered the square, I could see that the situation had changed. The crowd was denser with many more tents. Portable toilets and water stations were on the east and west sides of the square. Various institutions, schools, and hospitals had provided water trucks and ambulances to support the student movement. As I moved forward, I saw the students who were on hunger strike in front of their tents. Some had white towels wrapped around their head, some had written slogans on their bodies, and some were lying on their sides writing. Food such as bread and pickles were in the tent. Because the temperature had dropped sharply the last few days, donated blankets and clothes were stacked neatly next to the tents. More were stored in a centralized location. I could see that the protesters were highly organized and disciplined. Before I arrived, I had heard about the "Goddess of Democracy" statue that had been erected in the center of the square. I walked between the two underground passages on the south side of Jinshui Bridge and saw the statue surrounded by a crowd. It was white and four or five meters high. The wooden plaque in front of the statue said, in essence, that the republic established after the overthrow of the Qing Dynasty was in name only but had not achieved true democracy. The people yearn for democratic reforms: to move from the rule of man to the rule of law so that human rights are guaranteed, laws are upheld, and the economy is developed. The people want to be freed from the shackles of dictatorship, be rid of poverty, and backwardness, and thrive. I didn't bring a pen and paper, so I couldn't copy the words on the plaque, but this is the main content and spirit.

The statue of the Goddess of Democracy was erected to express the aspirations of the People. Since the power is not in their hands, this statue will be demolished sooner or later by those in power. However, the People will take power eventually. The demise of dictatorship is only a matter of time. This is the trend worldwide. No matter how hard dictators clamp down, they cannot evade their fate. When the time comes, we will build a Goddess of Democracy statue that is immortal and eternal.

A few days after the hunger strike started, the Chinese authorities responded. Zhao Ziyang, General Secretary of the Communist Party, visited Tiananmen Square to talk to student representatives and discourage the hunger strike. This signaled a shift in the authorities' hardline stance and made it possible that the stalemate would ease or even resolve. Sadly, within two days, matters took a turn for the worse. The diehards at the top of the Chinese Communist Party threw Zhao Ziyang out of office on false charges to usurp his military and political power so that they could deal harshly with the pro-democracy movement. Martial law was declared. Troops were sent to Beijing to crush the movement. Immediately, the entire capital was plunged into terror.

However, thousands of students, workers, and activists were not intimidated or discouraged. They worked to set up roadblocks at the main crossings to block the troops from entering the city. My house was at one of the intersections going to the western suburbs—West Third Ring Middle Road and Zizhuyuan Road. Trams and buses were set up for students, workers, and picketers to rest while guarding the intersection.

On the night of the incident, I was sleeping soundly when I woke up to the sound of gunfire outside. My home was on the 11th floor. Deep in the night, it's usually extremely quiet. The gunfire was clearly audible. I surmised that it came from the southeast. At first, the sounds were sparse, then they intensified, followed by the continuous sound of machine guns that mingled with screeching cars. We were terrified, not knowing what was happening. However, because the government had declared martial law, we surmised that it used force to suppress the students. We were sure that the unthinkable had happened. The gunshots continued for several hours and finally ceased at dawn. The suppressors must have been "victorious." This was inevitable since the opponents were unarmed students, workers, intellectuals, and the masses. They were killed because they could not defend themselves or fight back. I was so angry that I couldn't sleep. I hastily had some breakfast and went out to see what was going on. Crowds were already in the streets talking about what had happened. There were many hypotheses with no consensus. That night I listened to foreign radio broadcasts, as well as Beijing authorities' reports. The two sets of statistics on casualties were far apart. Judging from the intensity and duration of the gunshots that I heard, the number of casualties must have been extremely high. However, the actual number is still unknown to the outside world.

In the following days, domestic radio and television stations broadcasted for many hours about the "counter-revolutionary riots" and how the "riots" were "peacefully" quieted down. The government reports were full of contradictions and obfuscation. Even though they knew they couldn't deceive us, they had to continue the charade of deception.

Regarding this student movement, something else needs to be said. The pro-democracy movement was carried out by following our constitution, which stated that people have the right to demonstrate. It was enormous in scale, huge in number, passionate and enthusiastic, and surprisingly orderly. It was universally acknowledged that the participants were disciplined and respectful. In the latter part of the movement, I went out almost every day, walked around, and watched the crowds and parades. I didn't see any fights, disputes, or disorderly conduct. There were only friendly interactions. According to many people, during this time, crimes such as theft, robbery, assault, and murder were much lower than usual. That the pro-democracy movement was orderly was indisputable. As for "riots," the slaughtering of students and the masses were solely done by soldiers with tanks and machine guns. Unarmed civilians had neither sticks nor stones nor the intention to provoke a riot.

After the Tiananmen massacre, I was too upset to work on this partially finished manuscript.

After three months of rambling thoughts, I came to a realization: "the rise and fall of the country is the responsibility of every person." As a Chinese, I should take some responsibility for China's future and destiny. Don't pin your hopes on others, but take action and make a difference, especially during hard times. Don't get depressed. As a scholar, even though I am getting on in years, if I were motivated, I could still use my humble pen to fight against authoritarianism and expose our country's atrocities using my experiences, and play a small part in the pro-democracy movement. These thoughts inspired me to finish my manuscript, which I had thought of discarding. I reorganized and re-conceptualized the draft from beginning to end and finished it. I looked forward to seeing it out in the world. As for any dire consequences that could result, I was not concerned. As long as I could do my part, it was my great joy and the most meaningful thing I could do in my ordinary and bumpy life.

When I was in college in 1935, I participated in the 12.9 movement, which I still remember vividly. That movement invigorated people's hearts and morale and played a huge role in mobilizing the government's war effort against Japan. Now, this pro-democracy movement far surpasses that of the 12.9 movements in scale, time, significance, and influence. Future generations will discuss this movement at the macro level, such as its causes, influences, and consequences. However, the specific circumstances and details at the micro level may be few and even be lost. These details are indispensable because they could elicit sympathy and indignation. I was there, and since I'm writing this book, I'm including the details of what I witnessed. I ardently hope that the authoritarian system under the rule of man will give way to the democratic system under the rule of law.

    May dictatorship be eradicated forever!

www.ingramcontent.com/pod-product-compliance
Lightning Source LLC
Chambersburg PA
CBHW052052220426
43663CB00012B/2537